AF271190

THE MENTOR'S GUIDE

How to Be the Kind of Mentor
You Once Had—
Or Wish You'd Had

Revised Edition

by Linda Phillips-Jones, Ph.D.

It is no wonder, then, that when people tell us about the leaders who really make a difference in their lives, they frequently tell us about people who believe in them and encourage them to reach beyond their own self-doubts, to more fully realize their own greatest strengths. They talk about leaders who treat them in ways that buoy their self-confidence, making it possible for them to achieve more than they themselves initially believe possible.

— James M. Kouzes & Barry Z. Posner
Encouraging the Heart: A Leader's Guide to Rewarding and Recognizing Others

Cover Design by Tracy Nino

© 2003 by Linda Phillips-Jones, Ph.D. (Original copyrights, 1989-2000) All rights reserved. Published by the Coalition of Counseling Centers (CCC)/The Mentoring Group, 13560 Mesa Drive, Grass Valley, CA 95949, USA; Phone: 530.268.1146; Fax: 530.268.3636; E-mail: info@mentoringgroup.com. Call or write for ordering information and permission to reproduce limited sections for educational purposes.

NOTE: These materials cannot be copied. For additional copies of this *Guide*, please contact CCC/The Mentoring Group.

CCC101.01

Table of Contents

INTRODUCTION

Congratulations on taking steps to increase your skills as a mentor! As you probably know, mentoring is a recognized professional development strategy used by millions of individuals and thousands of organizations worldwide.

The Mentor's Guide is designed to help you have a successful partnership with your mentees. (Notice the plural, which can include both formal and informal mentees.) It should save you time, provide ideas to build on in planning your mentoring partnerships, and prevent some disappointments and serious errors. You might use the *Guide* in a formal mentoring program. Or you could apply what you learn to various relationships you set up on your own.

You have probably provided some informal mentoring or other development assistance to someone in the past. These training materials will help you build on and reinforce the mentoring knowledge and skills you already have as well as provide you with several new ideas, strategies, and tools.

This is a self-instructional workbook with application exercises at the end of most chapters. You'll learn most if you complete those exercises.

Watch for the following symbol:

 Exercise (a tool/worksheet to help you apply concepts to your situation and reflect on your progress)

Notice how the *Guide* is divided into separate sections:

Introduction
Planning for Mentoring
Building the Relationship/Negotiating
   Agreement
Developing Mentee/Maintaining Momentum
Ending the Formal Relationship
Additional Learning

You'll see quite a bit of *structure* such as flow charts, forms, and task lists. Many people find these very useful for managing their partnerships. If you prefer *less* structure, adapt the suggestions to your own style and relationships.

One key theme you'll see in the *Guide* is that your mentees (not you) ought to manage the mentoring relationships. Since the focus is on their lives and careers, they should learn to take this responsibility. You may have to help them master this process.

This *Guide* is part of *The Mentoring Initiative Design Package,* which also includes *The Mentee's Guide* and *The Mentoring Coordinator's Guide*. Numerous other mentoring resources are also available from The Mentoring Group. (See a list of products at our website: www.mentoringgroup.com.)

The series is the result of more than 25 years of work and draws from the following: my original 1977 doctoral research at UCLA on mentor-mentee pairs; ongoing study of hundreds of individual mentoring relationships as well as experiences in my personal counseling practice of 15 years; all The Mentoring Group has learned from serving thousands of organizations; and continual review of mentoring and related literature.

This is a completely revised version of *The Mentor's Guide*. It includes many new concepts and learning experiences.

A number of individuals contributed to the contents of these materials, and they deserve many kudos. Special thanks go to The Mentoring Group's core team: Dr. G. Brian Jones for his continued support and excellent help on all efforts; Vicki Bahnsen for her expertise and ability to solve impossible problems; and to Laurie Schell, Kathy Hamre, and Leigh Petersen for their limitless dedication and energy.

The Mentoring Group has learned much from a number of individuals. Our first big clients, Hewlett-Packard Company and later Agilent Techologies, mentored us very well. I especially thank Lisa Lion Wolfe, Patricia Chapman, Lynn Erickson, Clark Macaulay, Manuel Arellano, Paulina Mustazza, Bob Coutts, and Kathleen Barton (now with her own company and one of our consultants) for invaluable ideas on implementing mentoring in large global organizations.

For other early ideas and experiences, I owe tremendous gratitude to the Clairol staff, especially Ellen Anderson, for work on Clairol's National Mentor Program. Pat Harrison of the Women's Economic Alliance helped test the original materials in Hungary through a joint project with the U.S. Department of Labor. Additional innovative ideas came from Tim Kane at Lucent Technologies, Marjorie Sutter at Kimberly-Clark, and Pat Brown at Conoco-Phillips.

Sincere thanks go to many others for helping us modernize our thinking and practices in mentoring. These include Bridget Bakken, Jason Scovil, Dianna Jones, and Eddie Pate at Microsoft Corporation; Tracy Weber (who consults with Microsoft and others); Michael Smith at Young Entrepreneurs Organization; and Steve Conrad and his team at MediaPro Inc. The thousands who visit our website and send us e-mails or phone also provide wonderful continuing education for us.

I also want to thank mentoring consultants, Dr. Tom Rogers and Dr. Andrea Molberg, for their excellent insights. Dr. Robb Most continues to provide expertise in the area of mentor and mentee assessment. Final kudos go to Lynda Murphy, Nancy Zabka, and Cele and Linda Becker for helping me stay focused on my personal vision.

I hope you benefit from the materials and welcome any suggestions and additions you care to send. Congratulations on taking this important step!

Linda Phillips-Jones

CCC/The Mentoring Group
13560 Mesa Drive, Grass Valley, CA 95949
Phone: 530.268.1146 • Fax: 530.268.3636
E-mail: info@mentoringgroup.com
Website: www.mentoringgroup.com

Planning for Mentoring

MENTOR'S CHECKLIST OF TASKS:
Planning for Mentoring

> **Directions**: *The following are tasks or activities to complete prior to meeting with your mentee. Read through the* Checklist, *add items (if appropriate), and check an item as you complete it.*

	✓	
1.		Turn in required paperwork to your coordinator (if applicable).
2.		Read through **The Mentor's Guide.**
3.		If possible, obtain more information about your mentee.
4.		Reflect on your past mentoring experiences for insights to use in this new mentoring partnership. Complete and be ready to talk about **My Mentoring Experiences**.
5.		Look over **My Personal Vision** (consider completing it), review your **program application** (if you completed one). Be ready to talk with your mentee about potential development goals and activities.
6.		Read over the sample **Mentoring Agreement.** (You'll discuss with your mentee and perhaps adapt it and/or give a copy to the coordinator.)
7.		Think through what you'd like your mentoring partnership to do. Be ready to review and discuss your mentee's **Goals for Mentoring Partnership.**
8.		Pull together relevant information about yourself (e.g., resume or job history, current job description, sample of your writing, photos) to share. Ask for hers/his.
9.		Determine any limits you have (e.g., are you traveling a lot over the next few months? Are you caring for an ill parent?)
10.		Participate in mentor training activities.
11.		Other tasks: (*List and check-off.*)

MENTORING THAT MAKES A DIFFERENCE:
Initial Principles

Successful mentors and mentees have a solid understanding of mentoring and how its works. This article presents some of the current findings about mentoring.

Benefits of Effective Mentoring

When mentoring is done well, all parties benefit. Here are some examples of what each group gains.

Mentees gain opportunities to: observe and interact with successful experts; receive personalized feedback and encouragement; acquire and improve their knowledge, skills and attitudes; save time by learning shortcuts and strategies normally learned by years of trial and error; ask specific questions; gain practical resources and tools; and increase their network as they interact with mentors and other mentees.

Mentors have opportunities to: increase their mentoring skills, which they can use in numerous personal and professional areas of their lives; learn new technical knowledge and skills; indirectly "pay back" their own mentors for help received; increase their professional network; pass on years of experience; demonstrate their ability to recognize and develop talent; gain tremendous satisfaction from contributing to the development of capable individuals; and possibly gain fresh enthusiasm for their own careers and lives.

Organizations benefit from: being able to contribute to the development of competent mentees and mentors; increased commitment of participants to the organization; having another benefit to offer their members; and obtaining a recruiting edge.

Why Mentoring Works

Powerful things happen when a respected, experienced person shows interest in and goes out of his/her way to help another individual develop, especially when that individual is open to being influenced.

At Stanford University, Professor Albert Bandura has conducted research for decades on this impact. Three findings are especially important.

First, we do most of our learning from *observing successful and unsuccessful models*. In other words, we watch people's actions, see what happens to them, and then emulate (or avoid) similar actions ourselves.

Second, we respond well to positive reinforcement from certain people. That is, we learn *faster* and *more effectively* when we receive positive feedback from *someone we respect*.

Third, we learn best not only from positive reinforcement but also from having "mastery experiences." That means we leap ahead in our learning if we master something difficult.

Mentoring at its best incorporates these three factors. Good mentors allow themselves to be observed, and effective mentees make a point of watching and questioning them.

Effective mentors encourage their mentees through positive words—genuine timely praise. Effective mentees do the same with their mentors, which in turn reinforces the mentors to invest more.

Finally, mentoring partnerships in which the mentees set *difficult yet doable* goals and master difficult challenges not only learn a tremendous amount, but build their self-confidence in the process.

Can we learn without being directly involved with other people? Yes. Can we learn better with and through experienced people we admire? Absolutely! And we can learn more efficiently.

Research conducted by The Mentoring Group over the past 10 years indicates that people's lives change dramatically when they're mentored well. This can occur whether the mentoring partnership is informal or is set up between the parties on a formal basis.

Important Research

Before you read further, stop and do some important research on yourself. Turn to "My Mentoring Experiences" at the end of this chapter. Take a few minutes to look back on a relationship you had with *someone who helped you develop*. This could be a teacher, boss, family member, colleague, spouse, or other person who gave you special attention.

It doesn't matter if you ever called this person a mentor, but choose a *positive* experience. For a person who comes to mind, write words or phrases in each box: how your relationship began, what you *specifically* received from him/her, and what the mentor got out of your relationship.

As you'll learn in this *Guide*, this was a form of mentoring experience for you. Why did you consider this a positive experience? What does your learning suggest for any new partnerships you enter? Analyze a second relationship in which you were the mentee, or analyze a relationship in which you tried to help or mentor someone else. Keep this information in mind as you continue.

How Does Formal Mentoring Differ?

Most people are familiar with informal mentoring. Probably all have had some helpful developmental relationships in the past. Without using the term, they experienced "informal mentoring" from a family member, teacher, past boss, colleague, or other person.

This type of informal one-on-one mentoring is going on right now in your organization. It's usually a good thing and should continue. Here's what's different about the formal mentoring approach.

1. Partnerships are specifically arranged.

In formal mentoring programs, mentees and mentors are matched by the coordinator or a team either manually or with the help of computers. Prospective participants apply, are screened, and are linked with each other.

2. The partnerships are temporary.

Unlike informal mentoring relationships, which can go on for years and even decades, the mentoring relationships are designed to be short term. Each pair achieves specific goals and then ends or transitions into a different type of relationship.

3. Intentionally, the mentee receives most of the help.

The spotlight stays on the mentee throughout the entire length of the relationship. The focus is on the mentee's goals and development, not the mentor's. However, mentoring is a two-way street, and the mentor gains a great deal from the experience.

4. Pairs may or may not have "chemistry."

Unlike relationships that just happen over time, these are formed for specific purposes. Consequently, a pair may not feel much "chemistry" at first. Research indicates that chemistry is nice to have but not necessary in formal mentoring. What *is* required is expertise on the part of the mentor, mutual respect, and genuine willingness to share. In many formal relationships, friendship and "chemistry" eventually occur.

5. Partnerships are monitored and supported.

Usually coordinators informally monitor and keep track of all the partnerships. They phone, e-mail, or meet participants now and then to see if partners are meeting and how they feel about their arrangements and offer appropriate resources. Participants don't share their confidential conversations with the coordinator.

6. Mentees and mentors may participate in some activities designed for them.

Depending on the program, special learning, networking, and celebration events may be held for the participants and their guests.

Expectations

You and your mentee will have a number of expectations. Some relationships experience problems because expectations aren't met or even discussed. To prevent these problems and to help you with your planning, here are some expectations that are common and considered reasonable in mentoring relationships. (These also appear in *The Mentee's Guide*.)

What Mentors Can Expect from Mentees

In any formal mentoring partnership, you can expect your mentee to:

- accept the relationship on a temporary basis, for six-12 months or until one or both of you decide it's time to end it.

- meet with you as often as time permits. (Your schedule will probably set the pace.) The minimum to keep the relationship productive seems to be one or two hours per month, but you can meet more often than that. (With new hires, more contact is advisable.) In-person meetings can be supplemented with phone meetings and e-mail. These count as important mentoring times.

- ask for suggestions or advice.

- listen to you, apply at least some of your advice, and let you know the results.

- keep any commitments made.

- keep confidences between you.

- evaluate the relationship at various points within the agreed-upon time frame, considering what you've accomplished and what next steps to take.

What Mentees Can Expect from Mentors

At the same time, it's reasonable for your mentee to expect you to:

- have regular meetings by telephone, in person, or through on-line connections.

- provide sound advice on her/his development activities and professional development concerns.

- keep confidences between you.

- follow through on commitments made.

- help resolve conflicts between the two of you.

- provide honest yet fair and diplomatic feedback.

- evaluate the relationship at points during the agreed-upon time period.

Your mentee should ***not*** expect you to:

- provide him/her with personal introductions to other people until—and unless—you wish to offer them.

- spend more time on the relationship than you're willing or able to give.

- continue the relationship beyond the agreed-upon time period.

See the chapter, **Etiquette of Mentoring**, for additional ideas on expectations.

Now that you know some of the benefits of mentoring, why it works, and typical expectations, go on to read about how the formal process actually works.

MY MENTORING EXPERIENCES

Directions: Think of two people who made a difference in your life by what they gave or did for you. Write a few words in each column, and be **specific**. For example, did he/she teach you something, critique your work, give you a responsibility? How did he/she benefit from the relationship? For example, did he/she feel satisfaction or learn from you?

	HOW WE BEGAN	WHAT MENTOR GAVE	WHAT MENTOR RECEIVED
Person #1			
Person #2			

From *The New Mentors and Proteges* by Linda Phillips-Jones, Ph.D.

THE FORMAL MENTORING PROCESS

Your formal mentoring relationships will go more smoothly and impact you more when your partnerships contain a certain amount of *structure*, a process to follow during the beginning, middle, and end of your formal time together.

Based on our assisting thousands of mentoring pairs, we recommend the following structure. With informal mentoring, this process is more casual and can be implicit (not talked about). With formal relationships, however, it's important to discuss and come to agreement on the structure you use.

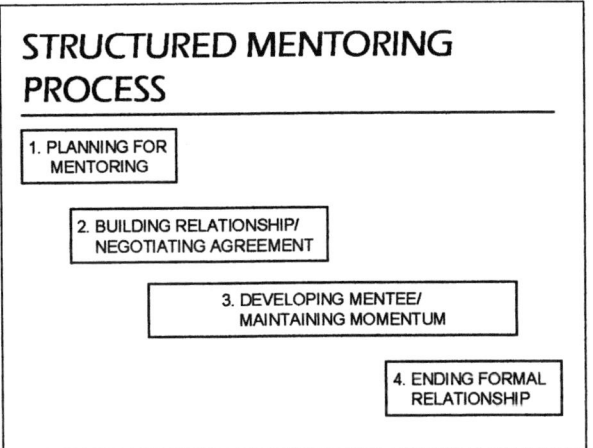

STRUCTURED MENTORING PROCESS

1. PLANNING FOR MENTORING

2. BUILDING RELATIONSHIP/ NEGOTIATING AGREEMENT

3. DEVELOPING MENTEE/ MAINTAINING MOMENTUM

4. ENDING FORMAL RELATIONSHIP

Notice the four phases, which occur over the six to 12 months the two of you agree to meet. The amount of time for each of the phases will vary depending on your needs and both your partner's and your styles.

You and your mentoring partner should do "process checks" from time to time to be certain your relationship is moving along satisfactorily. Let's now look at each of these four phases.

1. Planning for Mentoring

This is a new step recently added to the process taught by us at The Mentoring Group. Our work in recent years made us realize that the best formal mentors and mentees take a pre-step. They spend time—even before meeting each other—thinking about themselves and what they want to give and receive in these important relationships. You'll benefit from doing this, too.

This doesn't mean extensive, formal planning. But it does mean thinking about important things: where you've come from, where you are now, and where you want to go next. What vital lessons have you learned up to now? What's your vision for the rest of your life? What can you offer as a mentor? How could you help others excel?

The exercise at the end of this chapter and the next chapter, **Creating Your Personal Vision**, will help you jot down some initial thoughts. You can also go to our website at www.mentoringgroup.com and download some free tips. These will help you not only *find* the right mentoring partners but also be a dynamic helper.

Once you know yourself a little better and what you have to offer, you're ready to move into the next phase of the relationship.

2. Building Relationship/Negotiating Agreement

During the next part of your partnership, the two of you actually connect. You focus on getting to know one another, exploring each other's experiences, talking about other helping relationships you've experienced, and building trust.

Especially in "cross difference" mentoring (mentoring in which members are of different genders, ages, cultures, styles, work organizations), it's important to take plenty of time to develop a strong relationship. Don't rush too quickly into definite goals or objectives for your mentoring. Instead, take a month or more to explore possibilities.

Be sure to exchange contact information such as e-mail addresses and phone numbers. Ask your partner about when it's all right to call him/her. Talk about how soon you normally can expect a reply from each other.

Hold your first two meetings close together in time, for example, two weeks in a row. Other meetings can be more separated in time. Continue to schedule meetings on your calendars. If you don't reserve the dates, too much time will pass before you meet again, and the relationship will run out of steam.

> Effective mentoring can occur in as little as one to two hours of contact a month.

If you're in a formal mentoring program, check with the coordinator to find out the time expectations. You can divide this time into, for example, two one-hour lunches, four half-hour in-person get-togethers, or some combination of in-person and other contact.

> The mentee should take responsibility for setting up and managing the meetings.

Once your mentoring relationship is underway, start to nail down several agreements including the following:

- **Schedule**. Discuss the probable length of your formal partnership. If you're unsure about the relationship, suggest a "trial run" of three or four meetings so you can see if you're a good fit for each other.

- **Meeting Logistics**. Decide when and where you'll meet. If meeting in person, pairs usually find that offices are too hectic and prone to interruptions. Consider meeting at a quiet restaurant, in an empty classroom, outdoors on a park bench, or in some other relaxed setting.

- **Expectations**. Explore roles you picture for each of you. For example, do you want to be more of a sounding board than a teacher? Many mentors act the role of a "learning broker," helping their mentees find the information and other help they need. Or do you and your mentee favor a teaching or coaching role for you? Would you like to be an accountability partner?

- **Confidentiality**. The best mentoring relationships maintain confidentiality between mentors and mentees. Ideas, feelings, and plans stay between the two of them. Talk about confidentiality, including what is and isn't acceptable to share with others.

- **Feedback**. Come to agreement on how you'd like to give and receive positive and corrective feedback from each other. Ways to give these are covered in the chapter, **Skills for Successful Mentoring.**

- **Any Limits or Preferences.** Discuss your learning and communication styles so you can work well together. State preferences, limits, and even pet peeves. For example, is one of you a stickler for punctuality? Can you contact each other between your scheduled meetings? Does each of you prefer voice mail or e-mail?

3. Developing Mentee/Maintaining Momentum

The Mentoring Group recommends that your mentee choose up to three goals/objectives at a time to work on in your relationship. These *mentee development objectives* can focus on skill development, knowledge gain, or attitude change. Later you'll learn how to help your mentee choose these.

This is the longest phase of the relationship. During this time, you help your mentee progress in order to meet development goals and objectives. You mutually choose several development activities and maybe even a project on which to work. The chapter, **Development Activities and Plan**, presents many ideas for you to consider.

Here are several frequently used activities: talking together (e.g., about past experiences, goals, plans, skills, career paths, problem-solving strategies); attending meetings, conferences, workshops, and other events together (and discussing these later); working together on tasks; observing the mentor handling challenging situations.

You can role-play situations your mentee faces; exchange and discuss written materials (such as a document either writes, or an article one of you values); co-author a publication; and suggest meetings with other people (including persons who could be of help to her/him).

One of the biggest mistakes you can make is to simply say, *"Call me if you need me."*

The Awe Factor

Because of the so-called "Awe Factor" (your mentee could be in awe of you), he/she may not want to bother you. Relationships die because mentors think mentees aren't interested and vice versa.

Linda Phillips-Jones' research indicates that regular, scheduled contact is a must. Look at your calendars in your first or second meeting, and schedule your meetings at least three months in advance.

To **maintain momentum** in your partnership, try a number of ideas to keep the relationship interesting, productive, and mutually beneficial. For example,

- Plan to attend a special activity (such as a conference) later in the partnership.

- Change goals or add new goals to keep both of you motivated and learning.

- Give frequent genuine positive feedback and appreciation to your mentee. Show that you highly value this interchange.

- Be willing to deepen your conversations if this is comfortable for you. (See **Dialog Prompts**.)

4. Ending Formal Relationship

It's important to have **formal endings—** closure—in formal mentoring partnerships. Rather than letting a relationship continue and have no focus or letting it disintegrate from lack of attention, a formal ending will help both of you with this important transition.

Prepare for Departure Day in advance. *"We only have three more months in our formal mentoring partnership. What else do we need to accomplish?"* When departure is near, discuss several items:

- What you've accomplished

- What this experience has meant to both of you

- What and whom your mentee needs next in order to continue developing

- What each of you would like next for this relationship

Regarding what's next, both of you might choose to:

- continue the formal arrangement (see if your program allows it);

- change to informal mentoring (discuss your expectations);

- continue with a friendship (this might be difficult to implement); or

- celebrate, express appreciation, and part company with no future contact plans.

The Mentoring Group recommends some type of closing celebration between the two of you. Some pairs schedule a closing lunch or dinner. You could write an encouraging note summarizing what you've observed and expressing your appreciation. You might give a gift such as a framed photo of the two of you, a desk ornament, book, or a framed quotation.

You make the choice, but all of us respond well to the marking or confirming of important passages in relationships and life experiences.

On the following page, you'll see an overview of a typical 12-month mentoring partnership. Notice each phase and the potential activities in each. Discuss these with your mentee, and add or delete any.

For more details, look at the "Mentor's Checklist" that appears at the beginning of each part of this *Guide*. Before you go on to the next chapter, complete the exercise.

11

12-Month Relationship at a Glance

Prior to Starting the Relationship **Planning for Mentoring**	Think about your strengths, what you can offer, and any limits or requests you have. Complete **My Mentoring Experiences** and at least look at **My Personal Vision**. Be ready to react to mentee's tentative **Goals for Mentoring Partnership**. If in a program, complete and turn in required forms.	
Month 1 **Building the Relationship & Negotiating Agreement**	Complete training. Have first meeting using **First Meeting Tool**. Negotiate the relationship. Help mentee finalize **Goals for Mentoring Partnership;** complete **Mentoring Agreement**. Have second meeting. Use **Meeting Tool** to keep track of topics and progress. Communicate by e-mail, mail, fax, or voicemail as appropriate.	
Month 2 **Building the Relationship & Developing Mentee**	Meet at least twice. Check milestones. Have joint meeting with mentee's manager? Help mentee implement her/his development activities. Use other communication as appropriate.	**Implement Development Activities**
Month 3 **Developing Mentee/ Maintaining Momentum**	Meet at least twice. Check milestones. Use other communication as appropriate.	
Month 4 **Developing Mentee/ Maintaining Momentum**	Meet at least twice. Check milestones. Use other communication as appropriate.	
Month 5 **Developing Mentee/ Maintaining Momentum**	Meet at least twice. Check milestones. Use other communication as appropriate. Add or drop a goal?	
Month 6 **Developing Mentee/ Maintaining Momentum**	Meet at least twice. Check milestones. Use other communication as appropriate. Complete **Midway Review**.	
Month 7 **Developing Mentee/ Maintaining Momentum**	Meet at least twice. Check milestones. Use other communication as appropriate.	
Month 8 **Developing Mentee/ Maintaining Momentum**	Meet at least twice. Check milestones. Use other communication as appropriate.	
Month 9 **Developing Mentee/ Maintaining Momentum**	Meet at least twice. Check milestones. Use other communication as appropriate.	
Month 10 **Developing Mentee/ Maintaining Momentum**	Meet at least twice. Check milestones. Use other communication as appropriate.	
Month 11 **Developing Mentee & Ending Formal Relationship**	Meet at least twice. Use other communication as appropriate. Discuss transition of relationship (extend formal, change to informal, change to friends/associates, thanks and goodbye).	
Month 12 **Ending Formal Relationship**	Have celebration and express appreciation. Complete **Final Review** and share with mentee. If appropriate, complete **Program Evaluation** and give to coordinator. Sign up to be a mentor or mentee in next cycle.	

Using a Formal Mentoring Process with My Partner

Directions: *Write down your ideas about how you can add the right type and amount of structure to your mentoring partnership.*

Phase 1: Planning for Mentoring

1. (Example) Make a list of my expectations and hopes for this partnership.

2.

3.

Phase 2: Building the Relationship/Negotiating Agreement

1. (Example) Exchange resumes with my partner.

2.

3.

Phase 3: Developing Mentee/Maintaining Momentum

1. (Example) Propose using a written development plan.

2.

3.

Phase 4: Ending the Formal Relationship

1. (Example) Write a letter summarizing what I've gained from the experience.

2.

3.

CREATING YOUR PERSONAL VISION

A compelling vision and goals to reach it can help you succeed, be more satisfied with your life, and get the most out of your mentoring relationships. If you're looking for mentors, your thought-out vision and goals will help you know for what to ask.

As a mentor, creating or updating your vision will help you recognize your own growth as you help your mentees develop and reach their own personal visions.

Experts on leadership and personal development emphasize how vital it is to craft a personal vision for your life. Peter Senge, author of **The Fifth Discipline**, defines vision as *what you want to create of yourself and the world around you*.

Senge, Warren Bennis, Stephen Covey, career development expert Beverly Kaye, and others point out that a powerful vision can help you succeed far beyond where you'd be without one. That vision can propel you and also inspire those around you to reach their own dreams. *If you don't identify your vision, others will plan and direct your life for you.*

What does your vision include? Making a vital change in an area such as health, technology, the arts, or the environment? Raising happy, well-adjusted children? Writing a book? Owning your own business? Living on a beach? Being fit and healthy? Visiting every continent? Helping others with their spiritual development?

What are you good at? What do you *love* to do? What aren't you good at now but would like to be? All of these important questions are part of identifying your personal vision.

> *Keep away from people who try to belittle your ambitions. Small people always do that, but the really great make you feel that you can become great.*
>
> — Mark Twain

Part I. Conducting Research on Yourself

Before you write goals or even think about a specific vision, take time to research what you care most about, desire, and can do. The **Personal Vision** exercise at the end of this chapter will help you do this. The tool is adapted from many sources and is designed to help you think and dream a little. (Your mentee has the same tool in **The Mentee's Guide**.)

Notice that **Part I** is a set of questions to ask yourself. (**Part II** helps you put the research data into a Personal Vision Statement.)

Don't rush this process. Keep thinking about the questions and your answers, and talk about your findings with someone you value. When ready, go on to **Part II**.

Part II. Crafting a Personal Vision Statement

It's now time to pull together your research findings and summarize what you picture for yourself. Do this by writing a Personal Vision Statement.

Your vision must be *unique and appropriate for you*, so the following Personal Vision Statement is *only an example*:

> *I'm more physically fit, finished with my formal education, actively involved in two close personal relationships, worshipping and serving God regularly, having fun every day, and making at least 75% as much money as now doing work that I love.*

This sample includes *several areas of life* (physical, intellectual, social, spiritual, emotional, and career). It's a *picture* of how the person sees himself/herself and is written in the *present tense*, as if it's already happening.

Use **Part II** to synthesize the research you've done. What do your findings say about you? What *themes* keep appearing?

CREATING YOUR PERSONAL VISION, continued

Write your Personal Vision Statement in *pencil* if that's easier. Change it until it sounds and feels right to you. If you can't decide on one vision, write down *more than one* Personal Vision Statement. Make each Statement as *specific* as possible.

Once you've finished the exercise, share it with two people you trust. The more you talk about your vision and the rationale behind it, the more committed you'll become to it.

Stop and celebrate this important milestone in your life! Many people never take time to think about, much less write down, their personal visions, but you just did! Think big, and hold onto your excitement. Be ready to help your mentee turn his/hers into a plan of action.

EXERCISE

Part I. Personal Research

Directions: *Find a place without distractions such as a quiet table at a restaurant. Try to answer all the questions, and discuss your responses with someone you trust.*

What Brings Me Happiness/Joy	The Two Best Moments of My Past Week	Three Things I'd Do If I Won the Lottery
My Most Important Values *(Circle)* Having integrity Serving/pleasing God Being fit and healthy Having a nice home and belongings Leaving the world a better place Having fun Learning and improving myself Making others' lives easier or more pleasant Enjoying my family Being creative Others? (Add)	Things I Can Do at the Good-to-Excellent Level	What I'd Like to Stop Doing or Do as Little as Possible

15

Part 2. Personal Vision Statement

Directions: *Review your research data, and record your findings below.*

Based on my personal research, these are the main things that motivate me/bring me joy and satisfaction:

My greatest strengths/abilities/traits/things I do best:

At least three things I can start doing/do more often that use my strengths and bring me joy:

This is my Personal Vision Statement (in 50 words or less):

SETTING COMPELLING GOALS

Setting development goals that are desirable, feasible, measurable, written, and both work and non-work related is perhaps a mentee's most difficult task. She/he may be used to identifying work- or school-related goals. However, when it comes to personal development, the task can be—or at least seem—daunting.

Mentees often go to their mentors with only a *general idea* about how they want to improve. As a rule, mentors prefer that they get more specific.

Many development goals are too large or too small. Some are the right size but aren't particularly important or motivating. Almost none includes a way to measure success. Very few are written down, and some ignore personal in favor of only professional growth.

To avoid these mistakes—and potential feelings of failure—your mentee's development goals ought to meet the following criteria:

1. Desirable

What does your mentee feel passionate about? What makes him/her want to get up in the morning? What can be enhanced to keep this powerful motivation going? Conversely, what's keeping her/him up at night from fear or worry? What must change?

Within four months, feel more relaxed when giving presentations to clients.

Mentees' development goals should focus on *top priorities*. If they put care into writing a Personal Vision Statement, several priorities should emerge. It makes sense to set goals that impact the most important ones.

2. Feasible

It can be challenging to create goals that are realistic and attainable—without being too simplistic. *At most, help your mentee manage three goals at a time.* What's doable given his/her schedule, energy, resources, your availability and the months set aside for the partnership?

By the end of the year, learn Spanish.

Can your mentee "learn Spanish" in a year? Does he/she want to comprehend, speak, and write or only read? How well? What is she/he able to do right now, and what resources are available? Should she/he perhaps aim to comprehend and speak enough to take a trip to Chile?

Before next month's trade show, create a new website that receives at least 1,000 hits per day.

For this work-related goal, does the mentee have the expertise and financial resources to pull this off? In the above example, could she/he postpone the expectation of hits?

3. Measurable

How will both of you know when each goal is reached? What will success look like? What will the mentee have, do, feel, or know as a result of attaining the goal?

Assigning Numbers

A technique used by many mentors is to ask their mentees to assign a number (on a scale of 1 to 10) to represent where they are now and a second number for where they would like to be at the end of the period.

For example, if the mentee wants to be "more assertive with people," he/she might start as a 3 and aim to be an 8.

Here are examples of success indicators:

I feel more confident when I _____.

I've chosen my next career step.

My manager mentions a positive change in how I handle conflicts.

The scale says I've lost ___ pounds.

4. Written not Mental or Oral

Having a goal in mind or even talking about it is easier than writing it down. Yet, research studies indicate that writing down a goal (plus sharing it with someone else) dramatically increases the likelihood that it will be reached.

The mentee's written goal should be no more than 15 words in length, focus on one (not multiple) actions, and be recorded in a notebook, day planner, or computer/PDA file. The two of you can use the blank "Development Plan" in the chapter, **Development Activities and Plan**, to record the goals and monitor progress on them over the course of the relationship.

Help your mentee get over any fear of commiting himself/herself in writing. Although written down, goals can still be changed!

5. Focus on at least one non-work related area

If allowed in your program, help your mentee choose at least one non-work goal, one related to personal growth. This can be a goal related to any of the five life dimensions: social, physical, intellectual, emotional, and spiritual. These examples may help.

Add at least six people to my professional network. (Social)

Take my family on three trips of their choice. (Social)

Walk a marathon. (Physical)

Beat my brother in tennis. (Physical, Social)

Write an article that's accepted by a professional journal. (Intellectual)

Lower my public speaking anxiety from a 9 to a 5. (Emotional)

Attend (religious) services three out of four weeks/month. (Spiritual)

Three Other Factors to Consider

Once your mentee chooses and writes compelling goals, identify:

- any **obstacles** to reaching them (and solutions for overcoming these)

- **rewards** for goal attainment (What internal feelings or external "prizes" will help her/him make this happen?)

- how you can **encourage and help** with attainment and accountability

After choosing goals, your mentee can break the goals down into smaller, specific objectives. Or she/he can remain at the broader goal level. (Look at examples in the "Sample Development Plan" in **Development Activities and Plan**.)

Once your mentee selects goals and/or objectives, help him/her track progress. As needed, encourage your partner to change or add new ones.

The following exercise appears in **The Mentee's Guide**. Help your mentee use it to identify compelling (even if tentative) goals.

EXERCISE

Goals for Mentoring Partnership
(To be completed by mentee and reviewed by mentor)

Directions: *Write some goals you want to accomplish with this mentor. Make them desirable, feasible, and measurable. Be prepared to discuss them with your mentor, and if appropriate, make modifications after the two of you meet and create your* Development Plan.

1. The tentative personal/professional goals I'd like to accomplish with the help of my mentor:

2. I'd like my mentor to receive the following benefits from our partnership:

3. One year from now, we'll be able to say this about our partnership:

4. Other goal(s):

5. How can your mentor best provide the following:

   Encouragement –

   Corrective feedback –

   Help with your skills, knowledge, attitudes –

ROLE OF YOUR MENTEE'S IMMEDIATE MANAGER

As you plan a mentoring partnership, consider the role of your mentee's immediate manager. How involved, if at all, should he/she be in this mentoring partnerships? How could your role complement the manager's role with in this person's life?

> More and more individuals are creating their own "Personal Development Teams" or "Personal Boards of Directors" to get input on their lives and development.

The immediate manager, you, and your mentee's various other mentors could be part of such a strategy group. Your mentee might also have other assistants such as a personal coach, relative, or friend.

This team might meet as a group. More likely it will be a *virtual team* with your mentee's getting one-on-one assistance from each, then integrating learning on her/his own.

An advantage of this diverse team is that your mentee will have opportunities for *multiple feedback* and *advice* on strengths, development areas, goals, and development activities. He/she can *observe different leadership, communication,* and *decision-making styles.*

At the same time, this advantage presents challenges. The feedback, views, and guidance your mentee receives can be in *opposition,* leaving it up to her/him (with your help) to sift, integrate, and apply what's best. This is what your mentee has to deal with in the real world every day, so it's good practice.

Mentoring Outside a Program

Individuals can set up informal and formal mentoring relationships on their own—without being in any formalized initiative. If they do this, and if they believe the information will be well received, they can let their managers know that they're pursuing mentoring outside the group and gaining from it. This proof of initiative is likely to increase a manager's commitment to the person.

On the other hand, a mentee could have a relationship with a mentor (such as you) and *not mention it* to the manager. Some mentees prefer to do this if they meet with mentors on their own time or if they're working on goals not related to their current jobs. Others, for a variety of reasons, just prefer to keep the information to themselves.

If You're in a Formal Program

If you're in a formal program, especially at work, your mentee should involve her/his manager to some extent. The manager may have to nominate the person for the program, allow participation, and/or give release time to attend mentoring meetings and other events.

> The Mentoring Group recommends that individuals *don't* choose their immediate managers as their formal mentors in a program.

Your mentee can (and should) pull ongoing *informal* mentoring from his/her manager. But your mentee will develop even more when linked with a formal mentor who *isn't* in the same chain of command and who can be both objective and highly focused on the mentee.

In formal mentoring partnerships, mentees must feel comfortable sharing all kinds of topics. For various reasons, they may hesitate to do that with immediate managers.

As much as mentees may talk freely about personal vision and the future, they'll be *expected to deliver* on their managers' current organizational priorities and deadlines.

> One mentee described how valuable it was to open up with his outside mentor. *"My goal is either to get my manager's job or move to another division. My manager wouldn't welcome either piece of information, so it's great to talk about these options with my mentor. I can also admit how much I daydream."*

Some immediate managers are open, caring, and comfortable discussing just about anything, and eager to help their staff with growth, even if it means losing them or being replaced by them. Some want to be thought of as a formal mentor by their team. If this is true in an individual's situation, she/he should enjoy the generosity of that manager, and *still* choose a formal mentor outside the group.

Involving the Manager in a Program

If you're in a formal mentoring initiative, your mentee should have options. Learn any program expectations and requirements. Ideally, the two of you will have a say about the involvement of the mentee's manager and the mentee will manage the process.

- **Awareness level**

Your mentee might simply mention that he/she is participating in the effort, thank the manager for support given, and ask if he/she would like to keep posted on the mentee's general progress. How much, if at all, would she/he *like* to know about the partnership? The manager may be satisfied with occasional voice mails, e-mails, or a few minutes of conversation with the employee. Other managers want weekly updates.

Following this approach, your mentee will give periodic updates on goals and progress, perhaps sharing some activities you've done and some information gained while maintaining strict confidentiality with you.

The mentee could invite the manager to be more actively involved. For example:

- **One Initial Meeting**

The mentee might suggest that this manager and you confer *early* in your mentoring relationship. It's appropriate for your mentee to be part of that discussion. Here are possible things to discuss:

- ✓ the mentoring initiative in general, making sure all of you have the latest information;

- ✓ everyone's expectations of each other;

- ✓ your mentee's strengths; and

- ✓ your mentee's development areas.

Many mentees conduct these meetings on the phone, although some manage to bring the three people together face to face.

This manager-mentor-mentee meeting is a good time for the manager to be frank about what she/he has observed in the person, including both strengths and development areas. The mentee can share preferences about how you and the manager communicate with each other in the future (e.g., the mentee prefers to be there).

This early meeting may be the only one the three of you have. You then continue with your mentee with no additional formal input from the manager.

Finally, your mentee might invite the manager to participate *throughout* the partnership.

- **Ongoing Involvement**

You might have a second meeting midway through the partnership. This is a time for the mentee to report progress and get additional simultaneous input from you and the manager.

You might have a final meeting near the end of the formal relationship in which your mentee reports on the total experience and you all express appreciation to each other. Your mentee might also invite the manager to participate in the program's closing event, if offered.

Your mentee will be the best judge of the appropriate number of meetings, their purpose, and content. Get help from your coordinator if the two of you aren't clear what to do.

Final Thoughts on Mentees' Managers

Your mentees' immediate managers are in a position to be informal mentors, whether or not anyone uses that term. They have knowledge, contacts, and opportunities that can help your mentees develop and walk through doors. Help each of your mentees pull mentoring from these valuable people.

Look over the following mentee exercise.

Role of My Immediate Manager

(to be completed by mentee and discussed with mentor)

Directions: *Use this exercise to plan your manager's involvement in your mentoring experience.*

---

1. How much involvement, if any, would you like your manager to have in your mentoring partnership?

2. Does your manager know your mentor? If so, what's the connection, and how might this have an effect?

3. How could you keep your manager informed about your development progress and the non-confidential aspects of your mentoring relationship?

4. A successful first meeting of the three of you would:

   - be when and where:

   - cover these topics:

   - not deal with:

5. How will you handle contrasting advice or viewpoints you hear from your manager and your mentor?

6. Other considerations for involving your immediate manager and your mentor:

Building the Relationship/ Negotiating Agreement

MENTOR'S CHECKLIST:
Building Relationship/Negotiating Agreement

Directions: *Read through the* Checklist, *add additional items (if appropriate), and check each item as you complete it.*

✔

1.		Review the materials you prepared (**program application**, **My Mentoring Experiences**, **Personal Vision**) so you can be ready to discuss each with your mentee.
2.		Meet with your mentee (at the training event or by phone or in person) at _____ _____ (time, date, location).
3.		Using the **First Meeting Tool**, exchange personal information and why you're participating in the program.
4.		Take time to listen and start building rapport. Use **Dialog Prompts**. Find out some of your mentee's background, interests, and reasons for agreeing to be a mentee.
5.		Review your mentee's copies of **My Mentoring Experiences**, **Personal Vision**, tentative **Goals for Mentoring Partnership**. Discuss these, and make modifications in goals if needed. Share what's appropriate from your mentoring experiences and personal vision.
6.		Complete the **Mentoring Agreement** with your mentee. If requested, give a copy to the coordinator.
7.		Complete the rest of the **First Meeting Tool**.
8.		Schedule two or more future meetings with your mentee. These can be in person or by phone.
9.		Clarify what you agree to do before the next meeting.
10.		Other tasks: (*List and check off*)

SKILLS FOR SUCCESSFUL MENTORING

Effective mentoring requires more than common sense. Research indicates that mentors and mentees who develop and manage successful mentoring partnerships demonstrate a number of specific, identifiable *skills* that enable learning and change to take place. This chapter describes these skills and provides a tool for you to assess yourself informally on each skill.

The Identification of Mentoring Skills

For years, individuals assumed that the process of mentoring was somewhat mysterious. These relationships just happened, and "chemistry" had to be present. It was impossible (even somewhat sacrilegious) to analyze and describe the specifics of what was going on in these arrangements. Analyzing and putting names to behaviors would theoretically kill them.

Some people were able to find mentoring relationships, while many individuals were unaware of how to get started with mentoring and missed out on one of the most powerful development strategies ever devised.

Phillips-Jones (1977) studied hundreds of mentor-mentee partnerships as well as individuals unable to identify any mentors in their lives. The conclusion: mentoring was much more examinable and yet more complex than first thought.

On the "demystifying" side, Phillips-Jones discovered that effective mentors and mentees use *specific processes and skills* throughout their relationships. Further, the skills and processes can be *learned*, and relationships can be better—more enjoyable, productive, and even time-efficient—as a result.

Additional research by The Mentoring Group revealed that unless a fairly *structured process* and specific skills are applied, mediocre mentoring relationships occur. Not much happens, and participants become frustrated with their well-intended but haphazard efforts. Worse, disappointed participants become convinced that mentoring doesn't work.

On the positive side, when individuals use these skills and add structure, important, satisfying changes take place in the lives of both mentees and mentors.

> A skill is a learned, *observable behavior* you perform that indicates (to someone else) how well you can do something. The set of skills described here constitutes your overall ability to mentor and be mentored.

If you possess these skills to an adequate *quality* level—and if you use them as *frequently* as called for—your chances of having mutually satisfying and productive mentoring relationships will be greatly enhanced. The model on the next page illustrates the *shared* core skills used by both mentors and mentees and the *unique* skills needed by each group.

To help you be a more skilled mentor and mentee, look at the model, review the descriptions of these mentoring skills and the behaviors that make up each one, and start using the skills with the people in your life.

Core Mentoring Skills

Both mentors and mentees should utilize the following *core* skills in their mentoring partnerships.

1. Listening Actively

Listening actively is the most basic mentoring skill; the other skills build on—and require—it. When you listen well, you demonstrate to your mentors and mentees that their concerns have been heard and understood. As a result, they feel *accepted* by you, and trust builds. The way you indicate you're listening intently is by performing several observable behaviors. For example, if you're an excellent listener, you:

- appear genuinely interested by making encouraging responses such as *"Hmmm . . ."* and *"Interesting . . ."* or sometimes reflecting back (paraphrasing) certain comments to show you've grasped the meaning and feelings behind the message;

- use appropriate nonverbal language such as looking directly into people's eyes, nodding your head, leaning slightly toward them, frowning, or smiling where appropriate;

- avoid interrupting mentors and mentees while they're talking;

- remember and show interest in things they've said in the past (*"By the way, how did the meeting with your manager go?"*); and

- summarize the key elements of what each of you said.

Resist the impulse always to turn the conversation to *your* experiences and opinions and to find *immediate solutions* to problems you may be hearing. Listen carefully first; problem solve much later. If your mentors and mentees have a habit of immediate problem solving, see if you can help them be better listeners and problem explorers.

2. Building Trust

The more that your mentors and mentees trust you, the more committed they'll be to your partnerships with them, and the more effective you'll be. This trust develops over time—*if* your mentors and mentees observe certain appropriate behaviors on your part. To become trustable, you must:

- keep confidences shared by your mentors and mentees;

- spend appropriate time together;

- follow through on your promises to them;

- respect your mentors' and mentees' boundaries;

- admit your errors and take responsibility for correcting them; and

- tactfully tell your partners if and why you disagree or are dissatisfied with something so they'll know you're honest with them.

Particularly with cross-difference (e.g., gender, culture, style, age) mentoring, trust-building is crucial and develops over time.

3. Encouraging

According to Phillips-Jones' research, the most valued mentoring skill is giving encouragement. This includes giving your mentoring partners recognition and sincere positive verbal feedback.

THE MENTORING SKILLS MODEL

SHARED CORE SKILLS

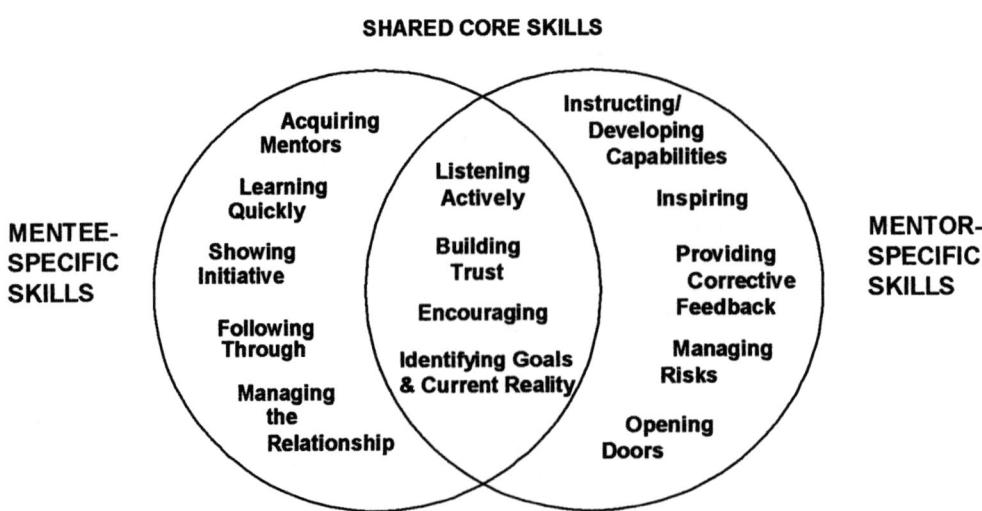

© Linda Phillips-Jones, Ph.D.

Mentors and mentees at several Fortune 500 companies revealed in interviews that positive verbal reinforcement—praise—was rare and even publicly discounted in their organizations. However, most admitted enjoying being recognized for accomplishments and abilities and receiving positive feedback—provided such attention was sincere and not overdone. Interviewees said they wished such behaviors were a greater part of their organizational cultures.

When was the last time you received too much praise? If never, you're not alone. Effective mentors encourage their mentees, which in turn helps increase the mentees' confidence and enables them to develop.

At the same time, successful mentees make a point of positively reinforcing their mentors, which serves to keep the mentors focused and motivated. Provide genuine, positive feedback to your mentors and mentees on a regular basis.

While there are many ways to encourage, and mentors and mentees can differ in the types and amounts of encouragement they like, you can:

- compliment your mentoring partners on accomplishments and actions;

- point out positive traits (such as perseverance and integrity) in addition to their performance and accomplishments;

- praise them privately, one-on-one;

- commend them in front of other people (being sensitive to any cultural and style preferences regarding public praise);

- express thanks and appreciation;

- write encouraging memos or e-mail and leave complimentary voice mail; and

- let them know how you use any help they give you.

Be certain that your praise and encouragement are sincere. In mentoring, err in the direction of *too much* praise, rather than too little. Some human development experts recommend a ratio of four or five praises for every corrective remark.

4. Identifying Goals and Current Reality

Whether you're a mentor or mentee, you should have a personal vision, specific goals, and a good grasp of current reality. As a mentor, be clear on and talk to your mentees about their visions, dreams, and goals. They'll be interested in your current reality (your view of your strengths and limitations as well as the current reality of situations within your organization) and want help recognizing theirs as well.

Mentees also need this skill. Before asking for help, you should know your tentative goals, strengths, what development you need, and the *specific* help you'd like. Discuss these with your mentors. The more aware you are of these, and the more accurately you can convey them to potential helpers, the more likely they'll be to assist your next steps. You can:

- know what's important to you, what you value and desire most;

- recognize areas in which you're able to perform well, very concrete examples of behaviors you can perform at the good-to-excellent level;

- identify specific weaknesses or growth areas observed in yourself and ones noted by others;

- set tentative one- to five-year goals to reach in your personal life and career; and

- describe accurately the reality of your abilities and situations.

Effective mentors and mentees are constantly fine-tuning this self-knowledge, incorporating new feedback and observations on a regular basis. Peter M. Senge (1990), in *The Fifth Discipline*, mentions these skills as part of "personal mastery," which he calls a journey, not a destination.

One effective individual, a former engineer who was currently a division manager (and a mentee in two mentoring partnerships), demonstrated her skill of identifying goals and current reality by writing this:

"My long-range goal is to be a general manager or vice president within ten years. My technical skills as an engineer and my skills (as an operations manager) are strong. I now manage 75 men and women. I'm weaker in sales and marketing."

"I expect to reach my goal by continuing to build our business, gaining some strong marketing and sales OJT in a temporary lateral assignment, getting coaching from my two—and probably future—mentors, providing formal mentoring to at least one promising individual a year, and hopefully, running one of our factories in about five years. My back-up goal is to leave and start my own company."

Model this skill by continually working on your own goals. Show your mentors and mentees how to take a less than ideal current reality and *pull* that reality toward their goals.

Critical Skills for Mentors

In addition to the core mentoring skills described above, mentors use several specific competencies in an attempt to help mentees develop.

1. Instructing/Developing Capabilities

Probably all mentors do some teaching or instructing as part of their mentoring. The skill is especially important in formal mentoring. This seldom means that you'll give formal lectures. Instead, your instructing will usually be more informal—from modeling specific behaviors to conveying ideas and processes one-on-one, in a tutoring mode. You'll:

- be a learning broker as you assist your mentees in finding resources such as people, books, software, websites, and other information sources;

- teach your mentees new knowledge, skills, and attitudes by explaining, giving effective examples, and asking thought-provoking questions;

- help your mentees gain broader perspectives of their organizations including history, values, culture, and politics;

- demonstrate or model effective behaviors, pointing out what you're trying to do; and

- help them monitor performance and refocus steps as needed.

A key part of your instruction is teaching *the mentoring process*. You can do this by making *process* comments—pointing out, naming, and otherwise getting your mentees to recognize which aspect of mentoring you're doing at the time—and why.

2. Inspiring

One skill that separates superb mentors from very good ones is an ability to inspire their mentees to greatness. By setting an example yourself and helping your mentees experience other inspirational people and situations, you can help them onto future paths that excite and motivate—even beyond their original dreams. Mentors vary in their ability to be inspiring. See if you can:

- do inspiring actions yourself which challenge your mentees to improve;

- help them observe others who are inspiring;

- arrange other inspirational experiences for them;

- challenge them to rise above the mundane and do important things in life; and

- help them recognize inspiring actions they took in the past and ways to excel again.

It's always tempting to tell mentees what to do and to have them follow in your footsteps. Your challenge as a mentor is to ensure that your mentees identify and pursue *their own form of greatness, not necessarily yours.*

Some outstanding mentors **use language—**stories, metaphors, and powerful phrases—to inspire their mentees. Is this a mentoring behavior you could hone during the coming months?

3. Providing Corrective Feedback

In addition to giving frequent and sincere positive feedback, effective mentors should also be willing and able to give mentees *corrective* feedback.

When you observe your mentees making mistakes or performing in less than desirable ways, you should be direct with your mentees, letting them know what you perceive and providing some better ways for handling the situations. It will probably be better for them to hear it from you than from others. This is an aspect of the mentor's protection skill, Managing Risks, described later.

One of the first things you can discuss with your mentees is *if and how* they'd like to receive this feedback. People are more willing to hear corrective feedback if they've given permission and know in advance it's coming. At the same time, you'll be more likely to give feedback if you're invited to do so. Attempt to:

- use positive, non-derogatory, businesslike words and tone of voice with mentees when their behaviors or products aren't satisfactory;

- give corrective feedback in private;

- give the feedback as soon as feasible after the performance;

- give specific (as opposed to vague) feedback on behaviors; and

- offer useful suggestions for them to try next time, offering to be a resource.

Use the Encouraging skill much more often than the skill of Providing Corrective Feedback.

4. Managing Risks

Another distinguishing characteristic of effective mentors is their willingness and ability to protect their mentees from disasters. One of your tasks is to prevent your mentees from making *unnecessary* mistakes as they learn to take *appropriate* risks.

This skill of Managing Risks builds closely on the core skill of Building Trust, identified earlier. Some refer to this risk-management process as helping mentees "step out on the branch, then fly when ready." You'll:

- help your mentees recognize the risks involved in actions, including some risks (and mistakes) you've experienced;

- make suggestions to help them avoid major mistakes (business, career, financial, personal, and other) in judgment or action;

- help them learn to prepare well, get wise counsel, then trust their own decisions and actions; and

- if requested in difficult situations, intervene as your mentees' advocate with others.

Mentees and mentors in many corporations have identified Managing Risks as an *increasingly important* mentoring skill.

Typical Risks

Your mentees probably face **business risks and career risks,** potential danger zones in which they could make large errors and possibly jeopardize their positions, careers, or organizations. Here are some examples:

Business Risks

Dealing incorrectly with customers
Missing deadlines
Underestimating project costs
Doing something unethical
Compromising on quality

Career Risks

Offending certain people
Taking the wrong position
Staying in a job too long
Not being able to sell others on one's own ideas
Failing to learn and improve

Some of these risks your mentees will recognize, and others only you—with your wisdom and experience—recognize. Still other challenges will seem more risky to your mentees than they really are. Offer to help your mentees identify and determine how to handle these risks with *recognition*, *prevention*, and *recovery* strategies.

---

5. Opening Doors

Mentors are usually in a position to provide visibility for their mentees. This means opening the right doors that allow them to meet people and to demonstrate to different audiences what they can do. *Research has shown that when mentors vouch for mentees in this way, their work is much more likely to be well received.* To open doors, you'll:

- put in a good word to people who could help your mentees reach desired goals;

- personally introduce your mentees to appropriate contacts;

- make certain your mentees' abilities are noticed by others;

- give your mentees assignments or opportunities that enable them to interact with important colleagues, suppliers, or customers; and

- suggest other resources to pursue.

You'll probably open doors for your mentees only when you believe they're ready to go through them. Since your reputation may be affected by your doing this, you'll first want to see your mentees as capable and trustworthy. Explain this process to your mentees as part of the development effort.

One mentee raved about how his mentor opened numerous doors for him. The mentor took him to two key meetings, allowed him to co-author (with the mentor) several papers, set up an opportunity for the mentee to make a very visible oral presentation to a group of decision makers, and nominated him for a highly competitive leadership development program within the organization.

Critical Skills for Mentees

In addition to the core skills described earlier, mentees need to be competent in several areas.

1. Acquiring Mentors

Becoming a successful mentee isn't a passive experience. In the spirit of career self-reliance, you should be very active in selecting and negotiating with *several* mentors who can help you succeed. Good mentors now have a wide choice of potential mentees, so you must skillfully handle the acquisition process. For example, be able to:

- identify a desirable pool of individuals who potentially can provide you with mentoring;

- actively search for several mentors;

- "sell" potential helpers on the idea of providing mentoring to you (in addition to—or as opposed to—others they might help);

- convey your specific needs and goals to prospective mentors; and

- negotiate the mentoring arrangements with your mentors, including agreements on goals, expectations, length of the relationships, confidentiality, feedback processes, and meeting logistics (includes place, form, etc.).

For detailed tips on acquiring appropriate mentors, see **Strategies for Getting the Mentoring You Need** listed in **Resources**. For more ideas on career self-reliance, read the excellent book, **We Are All Self-Employed**, by Cliff Hakim. (Also listed in **Resources**.)

2. Learning Quickly

Mentors enjoy working with mentees who learn quickly and take seriously any efforts to teach them. Typically, your mentors want you to be a "quick study." You should work hard at directly and indirectly learning *everything* you can as rapidly as possible. Try to:

- apply the knowledge and skills presented to you, and be ready to tell your mentors how you applied them;

- observe carefully and learn indirectly from the modeled actions of your mentors and others;

- study materials (those given by your mentors and materials you seek out) related to your development areas;

- integrate new learning into your conceptual framework for problem solving; and

- receive feedback nondefensively. (You should ask for specifics and be appreciative of the feedback. If your mentors have misperceived a fact, diplomatically tell them.)

As your mentoring relationships proceed and mature, you'll probably have ample opportunities to debate and disagree with your mentors. In the beginning, you should display a strong learning attitude, be willing to consider new ideas, and show an openness to be proven wrong.

Unclear about how to become a "quick study"? Try what one dedicated mentee did. She earned a degree in education and English then decided to go back to college and enter pre-med. The math, physics, and chemistry were daunting—her weakest areas by far. Not wanting to fail, she spent at least eight hours every day reading chapters, re-reading and marking them with a yellow highlighter, typing outlines of the chapters, and studying them alone and with study partners. At least two additional hours each day she found an empty classroom and wrote and rewrote math, chemistry, and physics formulas on chalkboards until she could recite them in her sleep.

A quick study? No, a slow study at first. But eventually she got it—and her 4.0. How committed do you think her professor mentors were to her success?

3. Showing Initiative

The newest approach to mentoring encourages the mentees to manage the relationships and show considerable initiative (see the skill, Managing the Relationship, on the next page). Even with this new trend, some mentors will attempt to lead the relationships and expect you to follow. Others will expect you to drive the process from the beginning.

Either way, they'll expect you to show the *right amount* of initiative. They'll observe the things you do *on your own* to develop. At times, most mentors will expect some following from you, particularly when your activities could have ramifications for them (e.g., approaching one of their valued contacts). As an effective mentee, you:

- know when and when *not* to show initiative;

- ask appropriate questions to clarify and get more information;

- pursue useful resources on your own;

- take informed risks (stretch beyond your usual comfort level) in order to acquire new knowledge, skills, and attitudes; and

- go beyond what your mentors suggest; that is, take their ideas and show creative or ambitious ways of using them.

Mentors vary in the amounts and timing of initiative they like from their mentees. Discuss this early in your relationships to establish preferences and expectations and to negotiate arrangements that work for all.

4. Following Through

These days, it's a mentors' market. Mentees who don't follow through on tasks and commitments are often dropped and replaced with mentees who do. You'll:

- keep all agreements made with your mentors;

- complete agreed-upon tasks on time;

- try out their suggestions and report results;

- explain in advance if you want to change or break an agreement; and

- persist with difficult tasks even when you're discouraged.

An informal poll of mentors by the author revealed that several were frustrated with mentees who failed to follow through on agreed-upon tasks. Some mentors even refused to enter new mentoring partnerships. They concluded that they were working harder on their mentees' lives than the mentees were doing for themselves!

5. Managing the Relationship

Even when your mentors try to take a strong lead, you're the one who should manage the relationships. It's *your* development, and you must take responsibility for its process and outcomes. To do this, you can:

- describe the general process of being mentored——how it works and why it's powerful;

- stay up to date with each of your mentors on issues between you, goals to reach, satisfaction with your meeting schedules, etc.;

- analyze the current status of your mentoring partnerships, and determine where to go next with them;

- prepare for the end of your mentoring relationships; and

- leave the formal relationships on amicable terms, even if the relationships continue on an informal basis.

Carefully track your mentoring relationships, and make suggestions as needed.

Final Thoughts

These are the critical skills needed by mentors and mentees for effective mentoring relationships. As a closing exercise to reinforce your learning, complete the mentoring skills self-assessment on the following page.

MY MENTORING SKILLS

> **Directions**: *Assess your potential to be a successful mentor and mentee by rating yourself on the following mentoring skills. For each skill, circle the appropriate number. Total the numbers for each part (I, II, and III), and read the interpretations.*

Mentoring Skill	Quality of Skill
	Excellent Very Good Adequate Poor

Part I. Shared Core Skills

		Excellent	Very Good	Adequate	Poor
1.	Listening Actively	5	3	1	0
2.	Building Trust	5	3	1	0
3.	Encouraging	5	3	1	0
4.	Identifying Goals and Current Reality	5	3	1	0
	Subtotal Core Skills				____

16-20 Excellent core skills; you could coach others; concentrate improvement efforts on fine-tuning your style

11-15 Very good skills; continue to polish those skills that will make you even more effective and desirable as a mentor or mentee

6-10 Adequate core skills; work on your less-developed skills in order to have better relationships

5 or under You'll benefit from coaching and practice on core skills; acquire training or coaching, and observe others who have strong skills

Part II. Mentor-Specific Skills

		Excellent	Very Good	Adequate	Poor
1.	Instructing/Developing Capabilities	5	3	1	0
2.	Inspiring	5	3	1	0
3.	Providing Corrective Feedback	5	3	1	0
4.	Managing Risks	5	3	1	0
5.	Opening Doors	5	3	1	0
	Subtotal Mentor Skills				____

20-25 Excellent mentor skills; you could coach others; concentrate improvement efforts on fine-tuning your style with particular mentees

15-19 Very good skills; continue to polish those skills that will make you even more effective and desirable as a mentor

10-14 Adequate mentor skills; work on your less-developed skills in order to acquire strong mentees and have better relationships with them

9 or under You'll benefit from coaching and practice on mentor skills; acquire training or coaching, and observe others who have strong skills

Part III. Mentee-Specific Skills

		Excellent	Very Good	Adequate	Poor
1.	Acquiring Mentors	5	3	1	0
2.	Learning Quickly	5	3	1	0
3.	Showing Initiative	5	3	1	0
4.	Following Through	5	3	1	0
5.	Managing the Relationship	5	3	1	0
	Subtotal Mentee Skills				____

20-25 Excellent mentee skills; you could coach other mentees; concentrate any improvement efforts on fine-tuning your style with particular mentors

15-19 Very good skills; continue to polish those skills that will make you even more effective and desirable as a mentee

10-14 Adequate mentee skills; work on your less-developed skills in order to acquire strong mentors and have better relationships with them

9 or under You'll benefit from coaching and practice on mentee skills; get training or coaching, and observe others who have strong skills

THE ETIQUETTE OF MENTORING:
Do's and Don'ts for Mentees and Mentors

et-i-quette: *any special code of behavior or courtesy*

— *The American Heritage Dictionary of the English Language*

An unspoken etiquette exists in mentoring relationships. Unfortunately, since it's unspoken, it's often unlearned, and participants end up, quite unknowingly and unintentionally, doing the wrong thing. This chapter is an attempt to make the "rules" more explicit. These rules are actually guidelines, since all mentors and mentees come to relationships with different styles and expectations. Ideally, one of the first things you and your partner should discuss with each other is the rules you'd like to use in your relationship.

As with all etiquette, the overriding rule is to make the other person feel at ease, knowledgeable about what to do, and valued. In general, this means showing kindness, flexibility, and appreciation, and using a combination of good business and social manners.

More specifically, there are several do's and don'ts that are usually followed in successful mentoring partnerships. Since mentees should show respect to their mentors, the first set of do's and don'ts is for them.

Suggestions for Mentees

Do

Take time to identify your goals.

Be considerate of your mentor's time.

Return phone calls and e-mails promptly, be on time. Let your mentor suggest extra minutes or activities.

Listen attentively to all (or nearly all) your mentor has to say. Store what seems irrelevant for some future use.

Be complete yet succinct in your comments and explanations. Ask directly if you're talking too much.

Seriously consider all advice you receive.

Show evidence that you've utilized the help to make your choice.

Show appreciation for every form of assistance your mentor gives you. Say thanks, praise him/her to and in front of others, write a note, etc.

Make it easy for your mentor to give you corrective feedback. Ask for it early.

Assume the relationship will be strictly professional.

Make only positive or neutral comments about your mentor to others. If you disagree with your mentor's behaviors or values, share your perceptions with her/him. If the situation continues, accept it or move on.

In formal partnerships, be prepared to move out of the relationship (at least the formal mentor-mentee aspect) at the end of a year—or sooner if agreed on by both parties.

Keep the doors open to return to your mentor for advice or other help later.

Keep in touch once you part company. Send a note or call from time to time to provide progress reports and say thanks.

Don't

Depend on your mentor to identify your goals for you.

Assume your mentor has unlimited time for you.

Tune out when the topic seems irrelevant to your immediate needs.

Ramble on, ignoring clues that you're talking too long.

Say *"Yes, but . . . ."*

Forget to share the outcome of the help your mentor gave.

Take your mentor for granted or assume he/she doesn't need this reinforcement.

Immediately defend or explain yourself, or worse, criticize your mentor.

Intrude into your mentor's personal life or expect to be close friends.

Talk negatively about your mentor behind his/her back.

Hang onto your mentor indefinitely.

Leave on bad terms.

Move on without checking back with past mentors.

Mentors also have some "rules" to keep in mind. You, too, can take steps to show respect and to put your mentees at ease.

Suggestions for Mentors

Do

Help your mentee take the initiative in your relationship. Be open to the mentee's ideas, discuss topics, etc. Help him/her learn to manage mentors such as you.

Respect your mentee's time as much as your own.

Be explicit about your own needs and limits (e.g., time constraints, style of interacting).

Always ask if you can make a suggestion or offer criticism.

Tell your mentee that you don't expect him/her to follow all of your suggestions.

Expect your mentee to move toward his/her (not your) goals.

Express appreciation to your mentee for help given you or other steps taken.

Recognize and work through conflicts in caring ways. Invite discussion of differences with your mentee. Ask a third party to assist when necessary.

Keep your relationship on a professional basis.

Make only positive or neutral comments about your mentee to others. If you disagree with your mentee's behavior or values, share your perceptions with him/her and get help if necessary. If the situation doesn't change, take steps to end the relationship, and try to find him/her a different helper.

Be prepared to end the relationship (at least the formal mentor-mentee aspect) at the end of a year—or sooner if agreed on by both parties.

Keep the doors open for your mentee to return in the future.

Don't

Insist on waiting for the mentee to suggest every activity and do all the leading.

Assume, particularly if she/he is more junior, that your schedule always has top priority.

Make your mentee have to guess or learn by trial and error.

Automatically give advice or criticism.

Assume your advice will be followed.

Expect a clone of yourself.

Take your mentee for granted or assume she/he doesn't need reinforcement.

Avoid discussion of touchy subjects or force your solutions in conflicts.

Move too quickly into friendship, if at all.

Talk negatively about your mentee behind his/her back.

Hang onto your mentee indefinitely.

End the relationship on bad terms.

Final Suggestions for Mentees and Mentors

Being involved in a mentoring relationship is a *privilege* for both members of the pair, so you should go out of your way to be gracious and thoughtful to each other. When you're unclear about what to do or how to act, ask your partner. The gesture of asking conveys respect for what the two of you are working to accomplish.

Considering Protocol

Directions: *After reading the tips on etiquette for mentors and mentees, make a few notes about how you could apply this learning to your partnership.*

1. Are any of the suggestions in the chapter different from what you're used to doing in a developmental relationship? If so, which are different?

2. What, if anything, would you add to the etiquette suggestions?

3. Which suggestions will be most difficult to follow? Why?

4. What can you do if you have a question regarding mentoring protocol?

DIALOG PROMPTS

Here are several conversation "prompts" and "deepeners" to help you in your meetings with your mentoring partner. Notice that some are *questions* and others are *statements*. Avoid using all questions or your partner will feel as if he/she is on the witness stand.

On your program application, you mentioned _____. I'd like to know more about that.

What would make this partnership an excellent experience for you?

What might make it a waste of time?

How should I refer to you and our relationship when I introduce you to others?

Tell me a couple of high points and a couple of challenges in your day/week/month.

(For high points) What skills, knowledge or attitudes did you use to help make this happen?

(For challenges) What part, if any, did you play? Is this part of a larger challenge you're dealing with?

Are you open to feedback from me? How would you like it? What should I avoid doing?

What talents are you most proud of?

What makes you laugh?

Tell me about some personal accomplishments that you're proud of.

What was the best working situation you've ever had?

What part of being a mentee/mentor do you like most? Like least?

What keeps you up at night?

What did you feel when you _____?

How would your friends/loved ones describe you?

How would your competitors describe you?

What do you hope to accomplish in the remainder of your life?

Tell me about a conflict you had. How did it turn out? What did you do that was effective? What wasn't?

What do you wish you had known or done 10 years ago? Earlier than that?

How did you decide to ___?

May I ask your advice about ___?

How could I be a better partner in this relationship?

What have I said or done so far that was helpful?

What wasn't particularly helpful?

How do you balance work and the rest of your life?

What would you like people to say about you on your ____ birthday? What do you hope they'll forget?

EXERCISE

First Meeting Tool

Directions: *This is a tool for your first meeting with your mentee. (For future meetings, use the* **Meeting Tool.***) Use this form to plan the meeting. Fill in what you can beforehand. To the meeting, take copies of your* **application** *and* **Personal Vision.** *Be ready to review her/his* **Goals for Mentoring Partnership.** *Discuss a proposed agenda, adjust as needed, and write notes as you proceed through your meeting.*

Agenda

1. Background information on each other *(Mentee has own form in* **The Mentee's Guide***):*

Name of Mentee _____ Prefers to be called _____

Best contact address _____

_____

Phones (day) _____ (evening) _____ Cell/Pager: _____

Fax: _____ E-mail: _____

Educational Background:

Professional/Work Background:

Other Information:

2. Our partnership will go until _____ .

3. Assistance (knowledge, skills, attitude changes, resources) mentee needs *(Go over mentee's* **Personal Vision** *and* **Goals for Mentoring Partnership***; discuss strengths/areas to leverage as well as growth areas to improve.):*

First Meeting Tool, continued

- Immediate:

- Longer Term:

4. **Mentee's greatest challenges** *(What's been the biggest challenge of the month? Is it part of a bigger challenge? What will it take to overcome it? What options does the mentee have?):*

5. **Specific assistance mentor can/would like to provide** *(Keep this general at this point.):*

6. **Other resources that may be helpful:**

7. **Our limits or constraints in this partnership:**

8. **Preferences for communication/feedback** *(Discuss how to avoid ambiguities and miscommunication; how to give each other feedback, and how much pressure from mentor is appropriate; bring up pet peeves; and discuss plans for contact, if any, between meetings.):*

    Mentor:

    Mentee:

9. **How we'll know we've been successful:** *(Discuss how you'll measure progress both on the mentee's goals and on the partnership itself.):*

10. **(In general) Best times/places to meet:**

11. **Dates/times/places for next meetings** *(Give priority to mentor's convenience; note date, time and location.):*

    •

    •

    •

12. **Action items to be completed before next meeting:**

    •   Mentee

    •   Mentor (if any)

Mentoring Agreement

> **Directions**: *This form is designed to assist you in establishing and defining the parameters of your mentoring relationship. Discuss the topics with each other, and write a tentative agreement. Remember, the two of you can update and modify your agreement throughout your partnership.*

This agreement will cover the period from: _____ to _____

Mentee: _____ Phones _____ E-mail _____

Mentor: _____ Phones _____ E-mail _____

Expectations we have of each other:

How often, when, and where we'll meet:

Beyond face-to-face meetings, other ways we'll communicate with each other and how often:

Any limits or constraints that will affect our interaction (time constraints, travel, etc.) and how we'll handle these:

Mentoring Agreement, page 2

How the mentee prefers to receive positive and corrective feedback from the mentor (direct and to the point, "sandwich approach," privately, etc.):

Our agreement for handling confidentiality (everything discussed between us is considered confidential or only things that are specified during our discussions):

Role of the mentee's immediate manager in our mentoring relationship:

Challenges we're likely to face and what we can do to prevent or manage these:

Other agreements, if any:

This mentoring agreement sets forth how we'll work together. We agree to commit ourselves to the mentoring initiative for the specified period and to make a good faith effort to resolve any issues that may arise between us during the term of this agreement.

_____   _____
Mentor's signature/date   Mentee's signature/date

Developing Mentee/ Maintaining Momentum

MENTOR'S CHECKLIST OF TASKS:
Developing Mentee/Maintaining Momentum

> **Directions:** *Read the* Checklist, *add items, and check each as you complete it.*

✓

1.		Help your mentee prepare a **Development Plan**.
2.		Continue to show appreciation to your mentee.
	2a.	Say thanks for specific help or consideration given you.
	2b.	Compliment mentee on his/her skills, knowledge, and attitudes as well as other things you observe.
	2c.	Take him/her to breakfast, lunch, or dinner.
	2d.	Pass on information that could be useful to your mentee.
3.		Continue to meet (in person, on the phone, plus e-mails) on a regular basis.
4.		Monitor and make changes, as appropriate, in mentee's development goals.
5.		If appropriate, recommend people for your mentee to meet and perhaps interview. Suggest clues on how to interact with these individuals. Ask your mentee to let you know how these encounters turn out.
6.		Offer resources (e.g., books, articles) you believe would be helpful. Suggest that your mentee look for resources on her/his own.
7.		If appropriate, attend key meetings (yours or his/hers) with your mentee.
	7a.	Determine both of your roles beforehand.
	7b.	Afterward, debrief the meetings with him/her, explain your view of what was happening. Discuss the dynamics of the meetings.
8.		Follow through promptly on every commitment you make to your mentee. (If you're delayed, let him/her know why.)
9.		As appropriate, provide some instruction.
	9a.	Share aspects of your "career story," including how you made key decisions.
	9b.	Teach specific techniques you have found useful in work with clients, customers, colleagues, and others.

		9c. If appropriate, ask your mentee to observe you performing the skills he/she is developing.
10.		Continue to give corrective feedback on your mentee's ideas and performance.
11.		Continue to answer questions about your organization's policies, procedures, culture, and politics.
12.		Offer coaching on a specific performance or action(s) your mentee must take, for example, giving a presentation.
13.		Provide feedback on the program to the coordinator.
14.		**Halfway through your partnership,** do an evaluation of your progress and the effectiveness of your relationship.
		14a. Complete the **Midway Review** and discuss it with your mentee. If requested, give a copy to the coordinator.
		14b. With your mentee, discuss what you both concluded from the review.
15.		Based on the discussion, re-negotiate any aspects of the partnership.
		15a. Review the status of your mentee's goals and development activities.
		15b. Together, modify former goals or add new ones, and note new development activities.
		15c. Negotiate a timeline, schedule, etc.
		15d. Make modifications in the relationship as needed.
16.		Other tasks. (*List and check off.*)

DEVELOPMENT ACTIVITIES AND PLAN

Your mentee will find it valuable to identify specific *competencies* on which to work. Later in this chapter you'll see a sample and blank **Development Plan** with spaces for her/him to write the competencies to work on in your mentoring partnership.

For each competency, help your mentee identify some *development activities* that will help him/her master it. Here are some activities your partner may choose to do.

- *Read materials* you offer or that are found by your mentee. Study and critique these, and present appropriate applications.

- Be prepared for fruitful discussions with you. Bring questions, decisions to make, and challenging scenarios to your mentoring meetings. Seek your ideas on these.

- Try to *observe you* completing various work-related tasks. As a debriefing, discuss what you were attempting to do. (See Structured Shadowing below.)

Structured Shadowing

Your mentee can learn a great deal from "shadowing" or observing you and others handle various situations. His/her learning is enhanced when the shadowing is *structured*, that is, discussed and planned in considerable detail by the two of you. For example, if your mentee wants to develop negotiation skills, and you're skilled in this area, he/she could observe you negotiate a deal.

Step 1. You and your mentee meet to discuss an upcoming negotiation meeting involving you and a supplier.

You describe past experiences with the supplier, objectives, desired outcomes, anticipated obstacles, strategies for overcoming these obstacles, and dynamics that could occur. Discuss your mentee's role in the meeting, including how he'll/she'll be introduced, how active he'll/she'll be, and appropriate do's and don'ts.

Step 2. You both participate in the meeting.

Step 3. The two of you debrief what took place.

As soon as feasible after the meeting, discuss what occurred and why, what actions worked, what might have been improved, questions your mentee has, next steps, etc. If appropriate, have your mentee do a follow-up task such as a reading assignment or observing another situation.

- As appropriate, have your mentee listen in on a conference call facilitated by you. Discuss the call afterward, and talk about next steps.

- Critique your mentee as he/she practices or gives an upcoming presentation.

- Recommend your mentee take a workshop or class related to his/her goals. Have him/her summarize what he/she learned.

- Role-play or do a dry run of an upcoming conversation your mentee faces.

- Join another mentor-mentee pair for a joint activity.

- Provide feedback on something your mentee has written.

- Include your mentee in one or more of your *key meetings*.

Ideas for Key Meetings

The consensus of many mentees in formal mentoring programs is that they get more out of attending key meetings than most other parts of their mentoring experiences. Attending these meetings with their mentors provides exposure and a greater understanding of the organization. Try to include your mentee in key meetings.

A key meeting is an important meeting your mentee wouldn't otherwise attend, e.g., regional or national staff meeting, quarterly business review, conference on a topic vital to you but perhaps new to your mentee, or executive sales call.

Make the key meetings significant experiences. This can include jointly selecting an appropriate meeting, preparing beforehand on what to expect and observe, and debriefing afterwards so that your mentee fully understands the dynamics

> and ramifications of what was said and done. (See earlier tips on structured shadowing.)
>
> As a means of providing exposure, introduce (and encourage your mentee to introduce himself/herself) to as many of the meeting participants as possible.

Development Projects

Many mentees find it beneficial to work on a development *project* during their partnerships. Projects provide both content and process on which you can coach and give feedback to your mentee.

The *purpose* of a development project is usually to expand your mentee's understanding of your organization's operations, develop his/her competencies, and help solve a business problem that will directly benefit your organization. The main purpose is to develop skills and increase confidence, *not* to produce a product or other outcome. Be certain that the outcome doesn't become more important than your mentee's learning.

Examples of Development Projects

Development projects can include: conducting a study, participating on a task force, creating a new design, and putting together a critical presentation. Here are some examples of projects done by mentees:

- Investigate some of the *comments* from an employee survey, and make recommendations for organizational changes.

- Investigate some of the *concerns customers and others have had* in reaching appropriate personnel. Investigate if and why they're true.

- Create or modify a productivity tool.

- Conduct a *strategic analysis* of a new business or research opportunity.

- Look into appropriate *compensation programs* for certain positions.

- Determine how to *champion* and get an audience for one of the mentee's *new ideas*.

- Provide *guidelines for experienced professionals* to become mentors of less experienced staff.

You and your mentee should discuss development ideas fairly soon in your partnership. Ideally, by your second or third meeting, your mentee will choose the competencies he/she wants to develop and explore potential development activities.

Development Plans

Research studies indicate that mentees learn and progress more when they have a written development plan to use in their mentoring partnerships. On the following pages, you'll find sample and blank copies of a development plan.

Encourage your mentee to use the blank (or a modified form) to identify: *development objectives, measures, development activities* (including a project, if appropriate), *timeline*, and *resources/support* on which you'll focus during your partnership.

Use the plan to track progress, and make changes as needed. If your mentee's initial plan proves inappropriate, suggest he/she throw it out and start over. *Remember, the point of the plan is to help your mentee develop and be successful!*

Finally, as you pursue your mentoring partnership, practice several "inclusive behaviors." In other words, help your mentee feel valued and respected in every way.

SAMPLE DEVELOPMENT PLAN

Mentee: _____   Mentor: _____   Date: _____

GOAL: By the end of 8 months, become a more effective project manager as judged by my manager, team, and an objective assessment

Development Objectives	Measures	Development Activities	Timeline	Resources/Support
1. Choose project management knowledge, skills, and attitudes to develop	• Prepared list of target areas	• Interview project management experts • Summarize ideal competencies of project manager • Assess my current competence • Choose 1 strength to leverage and 2 development areas	• All by end of Month 1	• Manager, mentor, other experts plus contact info • Project management assessment tool • Manager
2. Build competence	• I score 50% higher on the competency assessment tool • Manager says I'm improving	• Subscribe to journal; search Web • Shadow mentor and at least one other person • Take two classes • Study past project reports	• Month 1 • Month 2 • Months 2 & 3 • Throughout year	• Mentor • Funding for classes • Self-study materials
3. Successfully manage a challenging project	• Project is completed on time & w/in budget • I'm more confident managing a project (from 5 to 9 on 10-point scale) • Team members give me high approval rating	• Project tasks themselves • Meetings with manager & team • Self-study • Mentor observes me lead a team meeting • Re-take assessment tool	• Months 3-8 • Month 4 and 7 • Month 8	• Mentor • Study materials • Post version of assessment

DEVELOPMENT PLAN

Mentee: _____   Mentor: _____   Date: _____

GOAL:

Development Objectives	Measures	Development Activities	Timeline	Resources/ Support
1.				
2.				
3.				

EXERCISE

Meeting Tool

> **Directions:** *Make copies of this worksheet for your second and future meetings. Use it as an agenda, place to make notes, and record of progress. Identify one or more goals or topics for this meeting and be open to additional topics. Keep the notes in a file for reference.*

Date/Time _____ **Location** _____

Progress made/successes to celebrate:

Challenges *(situations and feelings about them)*:

Specific goal(s)/topic(s) for this meeting:

Key learnings from this meeting *(Use back of sheet as needed)*:

Follow-up actions:

    Mentee:

    Mentor (if any):

Next meeting date, location, and tentative topic(s):

STRATEGIES FOR STRENGTHENING MENTORING PARTNERSHIPS

Once your partnership is underway, work on building trust between the two of you. As you know, genuine trust takes time, and yet you can take several steps to enhance the process. Here are a few:

Ideas for Building Trust

- **Show your commitment to the person.**

Show up for every meeting, be on time, talk about how this is a priority for you, do a little extra now and then, and speak well of him/her in front of others.

- **Reveal personal information including mistakes you've made.**

Rather than trying to appear "perfect," describe some errors you've made and how they made you feel and grow.

- **Share your feelings**.

In addition to stating facts, mention your emotions (*"I feel excited," "I'm worried," "I was depressed when ...."*) Avoid *"I feel that ...."* (a disguised opinion).

- **Remember what this person said to you before.**

Refer back to other conversations. (*"By the way, how did your aunt's operation turn out?" "You mentioned xyz last month. I've been thinking about that and ...."*)

- **Refrain from criticizing others.**

If you criticize individuals, your partner will assume you do the same about him/her in other relationships. Objectively describe irritating or disappointing actions rather than discredit the persons who did them.

- **Do what you promise to do.**

Follow through. Bring the book, make the call, show up at the event, and stop using that irritating word.

- **Give honest feedback.**

Gain permission from your mentee to do this. Be direct yet kind in the process. You may be the only person willing to do this in your mentee's life.

- **Be clear on what you do and don't want communicated to others.**

When in doubt, double check to see whether something is confidential. (*"You're moving to Denver. Is that something you do or don't want others to know?"*)

- **Refrain from any actions that are unethical, immoral, or illegal (or could look that way).**

Nothing destroys trust faster than observing or hearing about such behavior. In fact, pointing out how you're avoiding these usually builds trust.

Deepen Your Conversations

Once you've established strong trust, take another look at the **Dialog Prompts** in this *Guide*. Try some of the probes designed to facilitate deeper discussions.

If you're teased about being a "reporter" or "talk show host," just laugh and say you're serious about wanting to know him/her even better. Share some of your personal situations and feelings. Always respect your mentee's limits on sharing such information.

Showing Appreciation to Your Mentee

Mentees seldom ask for thanks or appreciation—or even consciously expect them. Yet nearly all enjoy and react well to genuine appreciation shown by their mentors.

The key is that your appreciation is genuine. Mentees are quick to recognize perfunctory thanks, patronizing, and other insincere gestures. Here are several best practices of successful mentors.

- Be considerate of your mentee's time. Although your schedule usually takes priority, do your best not to cancel or be late for meetings.

- Write a letter spelling out ways you see your mentee developing and succeeding.

- Compliment him/her on accomplishments as well as character traits (such as creativity and perseverance).

- Leave a voice mail or send an e-mail that expresses how much you enjoyed a conversation or meeting. Try to mention something specific that had impact on you.

- Give a small gift that would mean something special to him/her.

- Smile and laugh when you're together. Comment positively on his/her sense of humor.

- Ask for and carefully consider his/her advice, viewpoints, and reactions.

- Follow-up on advice and suggestions that your mentee provides. Let him/her know precisely how it was applied and the outcome.

- Mention what you're gaining from this experience. Help her/him know it's an enjoyable two-way street.

- Invite her/him to a special event.

EXERCISE

Strengthening Your Partnership

Directions: *List three steps you could take to strengthen your mentoring partnership.*

1.

2.

3.

POTENTIAL CHALLENGES

No matter how much you want your mentoring relationships to succeed, challenges will always arise. Most of them will be minor and will naturally work themselves out. Occasionally, though, you may run into problems for which you need another perspective. Here are some of the most common problems and potential solutions.

1. Lack of time or energy for desired personal contact between partners

This is the most commonly cited problem of mentors and mentees. Mentors are busy, and so are mentees. Sometimes even finding an hour to spend can be challenging.

Troubleshooting. There's no pat solution for this ongoing challenge. If you or your mentee really are too busy for a partnership, postpone involvement until later. As the mentor, you *must* commit sufficient time for the arrangement.

The Mentoring Group's research indicates that effective mentoring can occur in as little as one to two hours of mentor-mentee contact time per month, although more is even better. In addition, your mentee must spend extra time applying learning, completing other homework, and planning next steps.

> Help your mentee become good at making the most of brief encounters. Help her/him collect thoughts beforehand and have questions and ideas ready.

Maximize time by thinking beyond face-to-face dialogs. Some strategies include: developing productive and enjoyable telephone meetings; going to one or more of your or your mentee's meetings (and squeezing a debriefing session into the trip back); going on business calls together; working side by side on actual project work; shadowing you for a typical day; leaving comments on voice mail; and finding other helpers who can also help your mentee develop competencies.

You can also stretch your mentoring time through attending activities on your schedule;

and having your mentee apply learning to situations between mentoring sessions.

2. Difficulty choosing mentee development goals and deciding on needed help

Most mentees struggle with their development goals/objectives. Many expect their mentors to identify goals for them. They haven't explored their personal visions and so have no idea what they want to accomplish in the next year or beyond. Others believe that stating specific goals limits them or that they have to come up with very well-worded goals.

Even if they have goals in mind, many mentees don't know what specific help to seek from mentors. They're not sure what's appropriate or what's asking too much. They may mention some vague desires such as "help with my career" or "how to get ahead in this organization."

Troubleshooting. Be kind yet firm as you push goal setting. Encourage work on a Personal Vision. Discuss the chapters, **Setting Compelling Goals** and **Development Activities and Plan**. Help your mentee change goals as needed; don't try to identify the "perfect" goal.

Establish yourself as a learning broker who can help with the big picture rather than as a content instructor or even a coach. Become familiar with the protocol of mentoring. (See the chapter, **Etiquette of Mentoring**.)

3. Mentors who push their views and ways

In an effort to be helpful, some mentors try to give too much advice and tell their mentees exactly what to do. They also try to manage the relationships themselves rather than helping the mentees take this responsibility. In the worst cases, mentors insist that their mentees do it the mentors' way and become offended if mentees don't comply.

Troubleshooting. Resist doing this! You're probably used to directing others and want to help your mentee avoid mistakes. Effective mentors allow mentees to manage the relationships and to take risks that sometimes lead to mistakes.

Encourage your mentee to be assertive about her/his needs. Offer ideas and don't be offended when your mentee does things differently.

4. Overdependence on partner

Mentees as well as mentors can lean too hard on those providing emotional support. Both can be manipulative and may take unfair advantage of one another's time and contacts. Effective, dedicated mentors can easily get burned out by working harder on the mentees' lives than the mentees are working!

In addition, mentees may fear striking out alone without their mentors. Mentees may feel let down after leaving an experience with a particularly outstanding mentor. Mentors can experience a similar emotional letdown.

Troubleshooting. Share your reactions and decision-making and prepare to end the formal part of your relationship. Be honest about your needs and limits, and negotiate all aspects of your partnerships. Monitor your feelings and actions throughout the cycle of the relationships, and ask for help as needed.

5. Conflict between mentees and their immediate managers

Managers usually want to be involved in—or at least aware of—their employees' development progress. If they know an employee/mentee is meeting with an outside mentor, the manager can feel left out and even resentful. He/she may even try to block the process or at least prevent meetings on company time.

Troubleshooting. Think strategically about the role of your mentee's manager in your relationship. Urge your mentee to involve the manager, even if it's just sharing some learning. Study the chapter, **Role of Your Mentee's Immediate Manager**.

6. Obvious differences between partners

The Mentoring Group hears many mentoring participants say something like this: *"We just can't click. We come from such different backgrounds that I don't think we're a good match."* They're tempted to drop the relationship and look for a better fit.

Troubleshooting. While some partnerships clearly won't work, most can produce good results despite or even because of differences. Meet at least three times before you decide to seek a rematch. Treat this as an opportunity to increase your competencies in working with someone different from you. See the chapter, **Cross-Difference Mentoring**, for additional ideas, and complete the following exercise.

EXERCISE

Potential Challenges

Directions: *Now that you're more aware of problems faced in planned mentoring, anticipate your own. List the challenges along with a brief summary of a strategy to prevent or resolve them.*

Anticipated Challenge	Possible Resolution
1.	
2.	
3.	
4.	

Midway Review

Directions: *Approximately halfway through your agreed-upon time together, meet with your mentoring partner to discuss your experience, and decide what next steps to take. If you're in a formal program, give a copy to your coordinator.*

1. Learning

   a. Examples of specific things we've done together:

   b. So far in this mentoring relationship, I've gained the following knowledge, skills, and/or attitude change:

   c. Other benefits I've receiving from this mentoring relationship:

2. Our relationship

   a. What I value about the relationship:

   b. Ways, if any, this mentoring partnership could be more effective:

   c. Recommendations I'd make to other mentor-mentee pairs:

3. General comments on the mentoring initiative or partnership

Ending the
Formal
Partnership

MENTOR'S CHECKLIST:
Ending the Formal Partnership

> **Directions:** *Complete these tasks when you're ready to* ***end*** *your formal relationship. Glance through the Checklist, add items, and check each as you complete it.*

✓

1.		About a month before you're ready to end your formal partnership, reflect on what your mentee has accomplished and what you have gained.
2.		Complete evaluation activities.
	2a.	Complete the **Final Review** and give to the coordinator.
	2b.	Complete the **Mentoring Program Evaluation** and give to the coordinator.
	2c.	Meet in person or by phone with your mentee to discuss the status of her/his development activities and goals, your partnership, and any "unfinished business."
3.		Follow-up your closure meeting with a note of thanks.
4.		Express appreciation to the coordinator, program team, and your manager, if appropriate.
5.		Attend program final event, if offered.
6.		As appropriate, touch base with your mentee in the future.
7.		If appropriate, seek another mentoring partnership, either as a mentee or as a mentor.
8.		Other Tasks: (*List and check off.*)

PREPARING FOR CLOSE

Sooner or later, your formal mentorship must come to a close. This allows your mentee to move on to other helpers. It also allows you to help other mentees. About one month before it's due to end, think about the transition.

Best Practices of Other Mentors

Don't let your partnership fade away and die from lack of attention. Prepare for the end.

1. Review mentee's goals and progress.

Complete the **Final Review** and the **Mentoring Program Evaluation**. Discuss your experiences with your mentee and coordinator.

2. Decide on the next form of your relationship.

You and your mentee have at least three choices about what to do next. Consider the following possibilities, and be ready to discuss them with your mentee.

- **Continue the formal partnership.**

If your program allows it and your mentee prefers, you could carry on with the same arrangement. However, you should still make a *transition* from the existing to the renewed relationship.

Review expectations and help him/her identify new goals. Should the relationship change in any way? How long should this next period be? Set another time to review status and make new decisions.

- **Change to a business friendship.**

What does a business friendship mean to you both? Will the relationship be more 50-50 now with your mentee giving you as much or more help than you've given thus far?

Will you socialize on any regular basis? Will your families be involved? Again, discuss parameters and come to agreement.

- **Say thanks and goodbye.**

As with the other choices, this is a perfectly acceptable option. Your mentee may get what she/he needs and find it makes sense to draw to a close, at least for now. Be sure to express your thanks and let your mentee know specifically what you gained.

3. Mark the close.

Consider giving your mentee a farewell gift or letter. Let her/him know specifically what you've observed, what you gained, and how she/he impacted your life.

Note Your Emotional Response

Recognize that you'll probably have mixed feelings about ending the formal part of your relationship. It's enjoyable to be an appreciated mentor. If you've clicked as a team, you may feel a gap and sense of loss. If this has been hard work or a challenge, you'll probably feel some relief!

> A mentor commented: *"At first I was skeptical, but this experience was far better than I expected. I'll miss getting together with her."* Sometimes it's hard to let go of an outstanding mentee.

Pay attention to your reactions. This learning, too, is priceless and will help you think through how you'll do it when you again take on the role of a mentor.

Consider Being a Mentee

Once you've been a mentor, you may recognize how you could benefit from being mentored. Why not consider playing the mentee role?

Chances are you've already been a mentee in the past, even if you didn't define yourself this way. How about using your enhanced expertise again?

Could you find a formal or informal mentor in your organization or elsewhere? Visit our website, www.mentoringgroup.com, to gain monthly tips on being an effective mentee.

Final Review

Directions: *Before the end of your partnership, take time to identify what you've gained. If requested, give a copy to the coordinator.*

1. Specific changes/growth in me as a result of my mentoring relationship:

2. Other learning:

3. Something I'll stop doing or do less of:

4. Something I plan to do/do more of in the future:

5. Recommendations to other mentees/mentors:

Mentoring Program Evaluation

Directions: *Your feedback will help improve the mentoring program. Near the end of your agreed-upon time together, complete the form, discuss highlights with your mentoring partner, and give a copy to the coordinator.*

Part I. General Questions about Your Partnership and the Mentoring Program

A. Your Partnership

1. How frequently have you met with your partner? How satisfactory was this?

2. What were two of the most beneficial development activities you did?

3. What new or improved skills, knowledge, or attitudes did the mentee gain as a result of this partnership?

4. What is the most beneficial change you identified in yourself as a result of your partnership?

5. What type of feedback or other assistance did the mentor provide that seemed to help most?

6. Have you found your partnership challenging? Why or why not?

B. The Mentoring Program

1. What was the main reason you decided to join the program?

2. What were your initial apprehensions about the program?

Mentoring Program Evaluation, continued

3. What improvements would you suggest for the mentoring program?

4. Would you recommend it to others? Why or why not?

Part II. Your Ratings

A. Separate Components

> **Directions**: *Please rate the following on a scale of 1-10 (10 = outstanding/most important) for their usefulness and benefit to the mentoring program.*

1. Communication about the program   _____

2. Recruitment/matching process   _____

3. Kick-off event (if held)   _____

4. Mentor/Mentee training   _____

5. Resource materials   _____

6. Support provided for you and your relationship   _____

7. Other (Specify) _____   _____

B. Overall Experience

> **Directions**: *Please rate the mentoring program overall. 1 = waste of time, 10 = one of the most valuable times of my life.*

Your overall rating = _____

Additional
Learning

OTHER MENTORING OPTIONS

Many individuals only participate in formal, one-to-one mentoring relationships in which the mentor is older, and the two individuals meet face to face in the same geographical location. As powerful and common as these formal arrangements can be, you can also consider other equally valuable—and less traditional—mentoring options. These include "enhanced informal" mentoring, distance mentoring, group mentoring, reverse mentoring, and cross-difference mentoring. The following descriptions, tips, and exercises will help you consider these newer forms of mentoring for your use.

Enhanced Informal Mentoring

Enhanced informal mentoring is taking the place of completely informal mentoring. Instead of leaving mentoring entirely to chance, organizations are taking steps to acquaint people with its value and the best practices that are emerging that make it work. On their own, individuals are entering into mentoring relationships that have more structure than ones they and others used to have.

What *Is* Enhanced Informal Mentoring?

Typically with this type of mentoring, mentors and mentees choose each other and aren't matched or monitored in a formal program. What makes it different from earlier "informal" or "natural" mentoring is that one or both partners:

- are acquainted with mentoring concepts and strategies and

- recognize the process as mentoring.

The relationship is therefore more focused and guided than it is in completely informal mentoring.

How You Could Use this Strategy

If you decide that you could benefit from mentoring, think through what you'd like. Are you interested in being a mentee? A mentor?

It may be that you would gain most from signing up for a formal mentoring initiative in which you're paired with a willing mentor or mentee.

In addition to—or instead of—a formal partnership, are you interested in one or more *other* mentoring relationships? Ones that are less formal and yet are beyond friendship and actually useful for learning and growth? If so, rather than leaving those experiences to chance, study this *Guide*, become knowledgeable about all aspects of mentoring, and craft an enhanced informal approach that works for you.

Particularly if the people you choose haven't had similar learning, you'll have to guide the process and educate them to some degree. You may decide to talk (or not talk) about mentoring structure with these mentors or mentees. The important thing is that *you have it in your conceptual framework* so that you recognize and influence such important aspects as:

- how to approach the other person or recognize when someone is approaching you;

- ways to build the relationship and establish trust;

- appropriate requests to make as well as boundaries to respect;

- typical stages to expect in the mentoring relationship;

- potential discussions and other activities to do together;

- when it's time to move on; and

- how to end or transition into a different relationship with the person.

Some of your enhanced informal mentoring encounters will be short term and still very valuable. Others will be longer and perhaps even take on a more formal tone at times.

Best Practices Used in Enhanced Informal Mentoring

Here are some best practices using this strategy:

- Own your development, and continually look for people who can help you.

- Recognize people who could use your help to achieve their goals and thrive in their lives.

- Without necessarily calling yourself a mentor or mentee, start using mentoring skills and processes with everyone you encounter.

- Read materials on mentoring and suggest that your organization make mentoring resources available in the library or learning center.

- Learn the new language and structure of mentoring, and how to pursue the mentoring you want. (See the booklet, *Strategies for Getting the Mentoring You Need*, listed in **Resources**.)

- Encourage your manager and organization to reward employees in their performance reviews for implementing mentoring behaviors. Help make effective mentoring part of "the way we do things around here."

Can you think of ways to use enhanced informal mentoring in your life and organization? The following exercise will help you apply it in your situation.

EXERCISE

Using Enhanced Informal Mentoring

Directions: *After reading about enhanced informal mentoring, make a few notes about how you can use this strategy in your life.*

1. What could enhanced informal mentoring do that perhaps formal mentoring could not?

2. What are some potential challenges of enhanced informal mentoring?

3. Who comes to mind as a potential enhanced informal mentor or mentee for you? How might you proceed with her/him?

Distance Mentoring

What is distance mentoring anyway? Is it really mentoring? How can anyone mentor someone in a different city? How can you build trust without being face to face? If you're considering a distance mentoring partnership, consider these questions.

Here's what The Mentoring Group has learned about this fairly new (at least by this name) phenomenon, which not only is here to stay but is a potentially powerful strategy for helping people develop.

What Is It?

You'll hear and see the terms *virtual mentoring*, *remote mentoring*, *telementoring*, *long-distance mentoring* as well as offshoots such as *eMentoring*. They all mean the same thing: a mentoring relationship in which the two parties (or the members of a mentoring group) are in different locations.

The participants rely almost exclusively on electronic tools (e-mail, on-line meeting software/platforms, videoconferencing), phones, voice mail, faxes, and mail. The parties may meet face to face one or more times during their partnerships, but most of the time they're apart.

Why Use It?

Studies of mentoring initiatives indicate that sometimes the most effective mentor or mentee (in terms of skills, knowledge, attitudes, experiences, or contacts) is located elsewhere. Mentor location is less important than these other factors.

For example, in Hewlett-Packard's highest level leadership development programs, high-potential, high-performing mentees are paired with people who can most help them excel. Those senior managers and individual contributors are often on the other side of the globe.

Microsoft does the same in its innovative career mentoring initiative. For years, HP has also had an outstanding e-mail based program for adult mentors and youth. The Association of Research Librarians and the Center for Health Leadership and Practice link partnerships across states and time zones.

Here are some more reasons to use distance mentoring.

- **Many partners travel extensively.**

Even if mentors and mentees are located in the same location, one or both may travel most of the time. Consequently, for most of the time they must use distance mentoring strategies in order to be successful.

- **The uniqueness of it lends focus.**

Distance mentoring provides, for many, the ability to focus more intently. Since time is typically limited, meetings are planned in advance, agendas are exchanged, and both "get down to business" rather quickly. When partners are nearby, it can be easy to cancel meetings, get caught up in chatting, or drift away from planned goals.

- **Many shy participants find it easier to communicate.**

Many partners find they can have deeper discussions when they aren't face to face. As one mentee put it, *"I can say things on the phone or in e-mail that I might feel a little funny saying to him in person."*

- **New learning occurs.**

Finally, being in different locations increases at least two types of learning. Having to use the tools and strategies helps participants get skilled at and comfortable with these technologies. It also acquaints participants with unfamiliar cultures and geographies.

> Working with the Veterans Health Administration (VHA), The Mentoring Group learned that one purpose of VHA distance mentoring is to acquaint future leaders (the mentees) with practices and traditions of different parts of the Administration as well as of the U.S. They hope that the familiarity gained from working with the distance mentors will make the upcoming leaders more culturally savvy and willing to be relocated.

Is It Really Mentoring?

Yes, provided the mentor is going out of his/her way to use an intentional mentoring process and set of mentoring skills to help the mentee identify important life goals and build competence to reach them. In addition, the mentee must receive and use the assistance she/he is given.

Best Practices in Distance Mentoring

Before you attempt distance mentoring, check your beliefs and feelings about this strategy. If you're stalling, you may need to make a paradigm shift in your thoughts and emotions. Choose to recognize it as a viable strategy, build enthusiasm for it, and find ways to maximize its benefits and reduce its disadvantages.

1. Formalize the Telephone

You and your partner should set up regularly scheduled phone meetings just as you would face-to-face meetings. That requires planning ahead to schedule a time, proposed length, and agenda.

Tips for Telephone Meetings

- Send an agenda in advance. Mentees can take the lead in preparing and sending these in advance.

- Note each other's time zones, and choose times that are most convenient for the mentor.

- Turn off computers; remove other distractions.

- Call (or be ready to receive the call) exactly on time.

- Have the agenda, points, and questions in front of you when you begin the meeting.

- Take notes and date them (keep them in a folder so they stay together).

- Send a summary of agreements. Mentees can take the lead on these.

In addition to planned phone meetings, mentees report great satisfaction in receiving spontaneous calls "out of the blue" from their mentors. These gestures *("I just heard about something you'd like.")* build inclusion and help mentees feel valued. Mentors also enjoy a few spontaneous calls with good news or compliments.

Make use of voice mail. Leave information *("I'm sending you a great article about the presentation I mentioned.")* as well as encouragement *("You did a great job of calming that disappointed client.")* and appreciation *("Thanks again for giving me that feedback on the class I taught; it gave me the confidence to teach again.")*.

2. Use E-Mail

As much as we all complain about e-mail, it's a tremendous and inexpensive night and day tool for distance mentoring. It lets mentors observe how mentees write in general and use e-mail in particular. Your observations could help your mentees in their development process.

- **Pay attention to confidentiality.**

As you know, mentoring relationships must respect confidentiality in order to succeed. Who will read your e-mail? What will you do with any printed copies? As a general rule of thumb, don't write anything you wouldn't want showing up on the front page of tomorrow's newspaper.

- **Discuss response time expectations.**

Talk with your mentee regarding expectations about e-mail responses from each other. As a general courtesy, it's best to reply within 24-48 hours, even if you say, *"Just want you to know I received this and will try to get back to you by ____."* What about instant messaging? Are you interested, or is this too intrusive?

- **Send short, newsy e-mails.**

Rather than saving up your thoughts, news, and stories for long letters (or the next formal meeting), try to send short, two- or three-paragraph e-mails. If you meet by phone twice a month for 30 minutes each, you might send at least one e-mail during the weeks you don't have meetings.

Keeping this frequency of contact will help you stay up to date with your partner on urgent, important, and even lightweight and humorous things. Since you won't be bumping into your partner in the hall and having quick on-the-spot exchanges, you want to find ways to pick up on some of these current occurrences.

Consider e-mail attachments and the items you exchange. If from you (a position of respect and power), your mentees will likely think they have to read everything and respond. Discuss expectations.

- **Always, always put your contact information below your name.**

Never assume that the other person has your phone number, preferred e-mail address, and even mailing address handy at all times. This rule also applies to **voice mails**: always, always leave the phone number at which you want to be called plus a couple of time options.

- **Decide together if you want to "enhance" your e-mail.**

Spend a little time thinking about how your e-mail looks and reads. Some individuals really enjoy using their software tools (bold, italics, underline, colors, different fonts, stationery changes). They say that readability is improved because replies stand out. Others see this as pretentious or at least a sign the person has too much time on his/her hands!

3. Send faxes

Sometimes faxes work better than e-mail. For example, if either of you is traveling, finding a computer and Internet access can be a challenge. The fax machine is also good for printed articles that you can't scan into your computer. In all cases, be aware that others are likely to see your documents, so be careful about confidentiality.

4. Use the Mail

The Postal Service, UPS, FedEx, Airborne Express, and others are good supplements for sending less urgent, heavier things, such as longer documents, audiotapes, books, and small appreciation gifts. Also, a handwritten note or letter mailed by you conveys the importance of the relationship.

Other Tips for Distance Mentoring

Be compulsive about regularly scheduled contacts. One sure way for your mentoring partnership to fail is by leaving meetings to chance or "as needed." Mark your calendars well in advance for meetings and other events.

You could experiment with on-line software, such as NetMeeting, for your meetings.

Some pairs use "couriers," acquaintances who'll visit the mentor's or mentee's location, to send something (a spoken greeting, note, or package). Sometimes it makes sense for you to have one or more local mentors in addition to distant helpers.

Make the most of distance mentoring opportunities! Do the following exercise.

EXERCISE

Using Distance Mentoring

> **Directions**: *List advantages of and concerns you have related to distance mentoring. Then, identify potential partners and what you expect to give and receive in this relationship.*

1. What advantages do you see in distance mentoring?

2. What concerns, if any, do you have about distance mentoring for you?

3. Who (or what type of individual) comes to mind as you think of possible distance mentoring partners?

4. What could you realistically give and receive in this relationship?

Mentoring Groups

Many organizations are linking mentors with small groups of mentees instead of, or in addition to, matches with individuals. These arrangements are called *mentoring groups*, *circles*, or *rings*.

> As an example, Domino's Pizza now offers both one-on-one mentoring relationships and group mentoring for high-potential employees at their Michigan headquarters. Senior managers serve as pair or group mentors. The Mentoring Group provided training for mentors and mentees.

Advantages of Mentoring Groups

Mentoring groups can provide the following advantages, among others:

- Small or very specialized mentor pools can reach larger numbers of mentees.

- A group format is often an efficient way to convey standardized information (such as best practices for new supervisors or career development tips).

- Mentees who are shy or uncomfortable about speaking up often gain courage from other group members.

- Groups can stimulate learning and produce motivating ideas that might never occur in individual pairs.

Disadvantages of Mentoring Groups

At the same time, mentoring groups can have disadvantages and face several challenges such as the following:

- Some people don't like to learn or share in groups. Some mentees (and a few mentors) find this venue difficult and even undesirable.

- Some mentees want individual time with the group mentor(s) in addition to the group sessions. This puts additional time pressures on the mentors unless they can be firm about saying no.

- Confidentiality can be an issue, even when members commit to keeping information within the group.

- Individual sharing time for each participant is less than it is in one-to-one relationships.

- Once a group forms and gels, it's difficult and, in fact, undesirable to add new members.

Suggestions for Group Mentoring

Because of the popularity of mentoring, groups are likely to increase in number. Here are a few suggestions for you if you decide to participate.

1. Consider being a part of a group along with being in one or more pairs.

2. Recognize the challenge the coordinator has in organizing groups. Be flexible and willing to try the mentees selected.

3. Expect either one mentor-facilitator or co-facilitators to lead your group.

4. Expect about eight to 12 mentees in a group. If the group has fewer than eight, you could lose critical mass if some drop out. More than 12 makes it difficult for members to get individual attention.

5. Be prepared to discuss general mentoring concepts, process, and skills as well as group dynamics. You'll learn how mentoring groups differ from business meetings and social groups.

6. Plan to meet once a month for two to three hours.

7. Expect to meet for about six months. You may have the option of renewing your commitment at that point.

8. Encourage mentees to be responsible for scheduling meetings and planning the agendas. They can rotate the leadership.

9. Suggest that mentees use the group as an accountability team.

10. Rather than holding freewheeling discussions, your group may choose a theme. Mentees will plan a topic for each meeting, offer some content, and have open discussion.

Examples of Group Themes

- Becoming a Strong Leader
- Career Paths at _____
- Communicating Effectively
- Balancing Work and the Rest of Life
- A book such as *We Are All Self-Employed* by Cliff Hakim.

After two meetings, we'll close the group, and new people must join during the next round.

If a member can't be present, he/she will call someone to tell the group.

We'll emphasize encouragement, ask if we can offer corrective feedback, and make that feedback as gracious and helpful as possible.

We'll resist giving advice. Instead we'll share our own experiences.

11. Mentees may hear content presentations from mentors, experts in the group, or outside experts. Remember, however, this is a *mentoring group*, not a class with speakers. Mentees should link new learning to their objectives and be certain that they make progress toward them.

12. Help develop a set of group ground rules, and make sure members understand and agree to them.

13. Share your insights with the group and encourage mentee members to do the same.

Final Thoughts on Group Mentoring

Group mentoring on its own or in conjunction with a one-on-one mentoring partnership can be a powerful experience. Join a group—or even start one of your own!

If you're participating in group mentoring, complete the following exercise.

Sample Ground Rules

We'll start and end meetings on time.

Everything we say stays in the group.

EXERCISE

Using Group Mentoring

Directions: *If you're a mentor or mentee in a mentoring group, use this tool to plan your involvement.*

1. The reason(s) I'm participating in this mentoring group/what I hope to gain:

2. Some rules or guidelines I hope the group follows:

3. Questions I have for the group:

4. Other ideas:

Reverse Mentoring

ave you tried "Reverse Mentoring" yet? This is the process in which the roles of mentor and mentee aren't what they seem. The person who most onlookers might think is the *mentor* is actually the learner or *mentee*. Here are some examples.

The Mentoring Group recently received an e-mail from a young college senior in the U.K. who was asked to mentor a middle-aged returning student. In this reverse mentoring, both had to contend with a wide gap in ages.

A senior sales manager with 30 years in the field is told he has to learn computer skills from the college hire who's just starting his career. A newly promoted army captain has to rely on an experienced sergeant to bring her up to speed on her new unit. In each of these reverse mentoring scenarios, the gaps include age, career experience, and position or rank.

With reverse mentoring, the combination has an unusual twist to it, and the gap (age, rank, life experience, style) between the two is generally large. Just as with all other kinds of mentoring, the "reverse mentor" has knowledge or skills that the "reverse mentee" needs. What's different is the uniqueness of the situation and probable discomfort of the two participants.

Here are several suggestions for you if you're considering reverse mentoring.

General Ideas

1. Spend time thinking through this atypical arrangement.

What do you believe is supposed to happen? Is this the best way for the mentee to gain this new knowledge, skill, or attitude? If not, suggest another arrangement.

2. Don't assume you can be a reverse partner without preparation.

Effective mentoring is both an art and a science. Be sure both of you are well matched, willing, and well prepared. Learn the formal mentoring process and details about reverse mentoring, and polish your mentoring skills before you begin working together.

3. Agree to speak frankly to each other.

Decide to be open about your expectations, concerns, and preferences for such things as meeting time, communicating, homework, and feedback.

4. Keep the arrangement short, and have a "trial run."

Recognize this is a temporary arrangement that will last a few weeks or months. Meet at least three times before committing to a longer relationship (or ending it). If it's clearly not working, talk with the coordinator about a different solution.

5. Check in with the coordinator.

Especially early in the partnership, call the coordinator to prevent small issues from escalating. What works and what doesn't? What improvements could you add right now?

Suggestions for Reverse Mentors

If you're used to operating on your own, mentoring only people younger or more junior than you, or being mentored by others, it can feel strange to be a reverse mentor. Most people find it awkward (at first) to teach or coach someone a lot older or with much more life experience or rank. Worse, it's possible that your reverse mentee isn't convinced you're a credible mentor.

1. Decide if you want to accept this opportunity.

Whose idea is this? Your potential reverse mentee's? Your manager's? Yours? Before you say yes, determine the exact purpose for the partnership and whether you're the right helper.

2. Imagine how your reverse mentee feels.

Even though your reverse mentee is older (or at least more seasoned), he/she probably has some fears about this arrangement. Will others look down on him/her? Will you? Can he/she learn what you have to offer? On the other hand, your reverse mentee could be excited about this new opportunity.

3. Prepare well.

Read what you can about being an effective mentor. Visit mentoring websites for resources, check your library for articles, and ask experienced mentors for best practices.

4. Spend time listening, and be patient with both of you.

Since you're the expert on something your mentee needs, you'll be tempted to spend most of your time lecturing, explaining, and "telling." Instead, be a learning broker who spends a lot of time listening, asking questions, being sure your ideas are being received and understood, and referring your mentee to other resources (such as books and other people) when appropriate. Be patient with your mentee and with yourself, especially if you're both new at these roles.

5. Don't expect a close friendship.

The arrangement is temporary and for a purpose, and that's sufficient. Friendship may or may not develop; don't expect or push one. Because of the differences between you that define this as reverse mentoring, friendship may not be appropriate.

6. Even though you're the mentor, show some deference.

Mentoring protocol calls for your mentee's showing respect and some deference to you, including your schedule. At the same time, out of respect for his/her years of experience, you'll have a better relationship if you, too, show respect and some deference. For example, ask your reverse mentee for some advice.

7. Help your reverse mentee manage the relationship.

Since it's your mentee's development and life, he/she should manage the mentoring relationship. This means setting goals, making sure you meet, and ensuring that the relationship moves along and ends appropriately. If your mentee doesn't know to do this, help him/her manage you and the partnership.

8. Use positive reinforcement.

Studies on human learning indicate that people learn best when they receive genuine positive reinforcement from people they respect. Make positive statements to your mentee that reinforce effort *and* goal achievement.

Suggestions for Reverse Mentees

A word of empathy: If you're accustomed to mentoring, managing, and otherwise helping others develop, it can feel strange to be on the *receiving* end for a change. It may feel even more awkward if you have a reverse mentor— someone who's a lot younger or less experienced than you are in your specialty or one who has far less seniority than you have. Worse, it's possible that he/she hasn't mentored anyone before and will probably do some things wrong!

The good news is that reverse mentees report learning a great deal from this unusual opportunity. Does your prospective mentor have knowledge or skills you don't have but need? In addition to learning these, you can help this reverse mentor learn how to mentor mature people like you.

Reverse mentoring includes challenges. Here are some ideas to help you handle them and (as all good mentees do) *pull the mentoring you need* whether or not your reverse mentor is adept at his/her new role.

1. Decide if you really want to participate in reverse mentoring.

If you resist, the relationship won't work. Make a decision about whether or not you're going to be an enthusiastic partner.

2. Imagine your reverse mentor's apprehension.

It's possible that he/she is nervous about this partnership, eager to do a good job, and unsure how to work with you. Find ways to put him/her at ease.

3. Follow proper mentoring protocol.

Although you're the more senior person in terms of age, life experience, and possibly rank or position, this person is your mentor. Mentoring protocol calls for your showing respect, putting his/her schedule first, expressing appreciation, and trying his/her suggestions.

4. Expect some rough edges and mistakes.

Your reverse mentor may be new to the whole concept of mentoring. She/he may proceed too quickly or too slowly, be overly critical, or hold back on praising you. Be as patient as you can, and speak up if any actions are clearly inappropriate.

5. Help your reverse mentor learn how to mentor you.

Even if she/he has mentored others, you're a unique reverse mentee. Let your mentor know how you learn best, what's helping you, what isn't, and ideas you'd like to try.

6. Fight your urge to be critical or take over the process.

Trust that your mentor knows her/his subject and will succeed in getting you up to speed. You can gently offer suggestions here and there; just don't take over.

7. Pass on your suggestions and insights to improve reverse mentoring.

Let your organization know what you're learning about reverse mentoring. Tell us at The Mentoring Group so we can increase our expertise on this topic and help others with their reverse relationships.

To reinforce your learning, complete the following exercise.

EXERCISE

Using Reverse Mentoring

> **Directions:** *Picture yourself as a reverse mentor, reverse mentee, or both. Answer the following questions to help you successfully carry out those roles.*

1. (As a **reverse mentor**) What expertise do you have that you could share with someone who's older than you, in a more senior position, or with more life experience than you have?

2. (As a **reverse mentor**) What challenges do you anticipate having with a reverse mentee? How could you prevent or overcome these?

3. (As a **reverse mentee**) What younger person (or person in a more junior position than you) has some knowledge, skills, or attitudes that you'd like to develop? How could you establish a reverse mentoring partnership with her/him?

4. (As a **reverse mentee**) What challenges do you anticipate having with a reverse mentor? How could you prevent or overcome these?

Cross-Difference Mentoring

Have you been asked to mentor a mentee who seems very different from you? Do you wonder what mentoring you could provide and at the same time dread making a mistake with this individual?

Or do you have the chance to be mentored by a person who differs from you in obvious ways and have some qualms about making that relationship work?

The Mentoring Group calls this type of mentoring "cross-difference mentoring." While mentors and mentees *always* differ in some ways, when the differences seem particularly large, we give it this name.

You may recognize *one* key difference such as race, age, culture, language, religion, style, job function, gender, or upbringing. Or you could find differences on *several* dimensions. Your first instinct when this happens is probably to say, *"I want somebody else!"*

On the other hand, you could see cross-difference mentoring as an **exciting chance to experience and learn something new**. In this chapter, you'll gain ideas to consider as you venture across differences. Let's start by recognizing what could be standing in the way of your comfort and effectiveness.

Obstacles in Cross-Difference Mentoring

1. Negative stereotypes

You, like all of us, could be unconsciously holding onto some unfair generalities about a group. *They're slow, pushy, selfish, silly, weird.* You could be skeptical: *"What's his/her real agenda?"* Overcoming mindsets we've had from childhood, perhaps from our parents, or from even one negative example we've encountered is a major challenge.

2. Difficulty identifying with him/her

Especially at first, we think we're totally different: *"I can't see any of me in her/him."*

The more pronounced the differences, when nothing is done to bridge the gap, the slower the bonding.

3. Scrutiny by others

Perhaps in your organization, even if diversity and inclusion are valued, *some* cross-difference mentoring relationships are still **rare** and **therefore are noticeable**. People focus on and even scrutinize them, which may make you feel uncomfortable.

4. Resentment by peers

Others may act jealous or imply that a mentee doesn't deserve the benefits he/she is getting. One mentor commented, *"I tried very hard to be available to all the individuals in the department. But I invariably got criticized if I gave more mentoring to one person."*

5. "Protective Hesitation"

David Thomas, in an April 2001 **Harvard Business Review** article, uses this concept. It means that the two of you are likely to treat the relationship as more fragile than other relationships you have. You may be less willing to open up about sensitive issues and be afraid of confrontation because you don't want to offend or be thought of as anti-____ (*fill in the blank*).

6. Actual Mistakes

Unless you've had lots of experience working with someone with these characteristics (and even if you have), you're likely to make real mistakes. You really will say or do some wrong things!

Lois Zachary (2000) talks about cross-cultural differences in her book, **The Mentor's Guide: Facilitating Effective Learning Relationships**. You can make errors when you assume the two of you think the same and value the same rules of protocol, time and punctuality, spacial distance, authority figures (including mentors), decision-making, appropriate humor, etc. If you've made a mistake in the past and suffered the consequences, you're likely hesitant to venture there again.

These challenges aren't small. However, reflecting on this list, adding to it, asking yourself when and how you experienced these hurdles, and sharing with others about those experiences will make you a better mentor and mentee. The next key step is to take new risks to cancel old paradigms and look differently at cross-difference opportunities.

Benefits of Cross-Difference Mentoring

Research studies support many **benefits** of cross-difference mentoring.

Cross-racial. In that same *Harvard Business Review* article by Thomas, he states emphatically that people of color who advance the furthest all have a network of developmental relationships including mentors from their **own race and from other races**. A doctoral study of Asian professional women by Naomi S. Brown (1995) lends support for finding mentors who are from the **dominant (Caucasian) culture**.

Cross-gender. Numerous studies report benefits of females being mentored by males. For example, Ann Thompson Moore (1995), in a doctoral study of highly successful women in business, revealed that almost all had male mentors who increased the mentees' confidence and taught valuable career lessons. In another doctoral study of successful women in the U.S. Government, Linda C. Tysl (1993) found that although several ran into challenges with male mentors, they reported high satisfaction with (and learning from) their mentoring relationships. The Mentoring Group has found anecdotal evidence of successful **mentoring of males by females**. Many reported that their female mentors were more committed and willing to share experiences than some of their male mentors.

Cross-styles. Research on mentors and mentees with different **styles** is mixed. The Mentoring Group's general observation is that mentees will learn more (and be even more ready for the real world) when they meet the challenge of being mentored by people with different styles. Mentors will also stretch as a result of these relationships.

The payoffs of cross-difference mentoring are high. You and your partner stand to gain in many ways if you can meet the challenge of crossing and celebrating your differences.

Best Practices in Cross-Difference Mentoring

Here are some **best practices** of mentors and mentees who have succeeded:

1. **Become culturally self-aware**.

Know your own values and assumptions that someone not from your culture (or group) might not readily understand. Be ready to help others learn.

2. **Know your biases and prejudices**.

Determine where they came from, and be open to changing them.

3. **Discuss differences**.

Rather than pretend you and your mentors and mentees are the same, **openly bring up** the topic of differences. Regularly **talk about** what you're observing and experiencing.

4. **Look for commonalities**.

Don't force this, but start to recognize where you might have **similar thoughts and feelings**, work- and non-work interests, goals for your futures, hopes for your loved ones.

5. **Work on trust**.

Building trust will take longer, but you can **enhance it** in the following ways:

- Convey the message that **you want to be in this relationship**; you're looking forward to it. It has many benefits for you.

- Mention any **experience** you've had (or not had) working with persons with this background. Reveal mistakes you've made.

- Let them know you want to **learn** about them as *individuals,* and also learn about situations and challenges faced by this *group.* Don't

75

assume they agree with all beliefs or practices of others in the group.

- Do the **usual trust-building** steps: keep your promises; keep confidences; don't talk badly about anyone else in front of each other.

- Pay **special attention to language** and meanings of words; you may not be communicating.

6. **Learn all you can about your mentees' or mentors' worlds**.

   Read books and articles. Ask if you can go with them to events that will help you learn.

7. **Don't treat the relationship as fragile**.

   Use sensitivity and good manners, but agree to be open and frank with each other.

8. **As a mentor, help your mentees succeed**.

   - *Assume* they'll be successful. (Allow the Self-Fulfilling Prophecy to work.)

   - Help them develop critical skills, knowledge, and attitudes needed to get ahead.

   - Confront people who make unfair remarks about them or your relationships.

- Recognize their good ideas in meetings, and showcase their abilities.

- When they're ready, give them high-trust, high-visibility assignments.

- Help them build networks that will contribute to their success. Urge them to find mentors and other personal connections from both dominant and minority groups.

- Accept the fact that you'll make mistakes, *and* you'll learn from them.

- Consider finding mentors of your own who can help you be more effective with cross-difference mentees.

9. **As a mentee**:

   - Take the risk of finding partners with many different backgrounds.

   - Make it easy for your mentors to ask you questions, learn your views, and admit when they're confused or frustrated.

   - Invite honest feedback; stay non-defensive.

   - Show appreciation.

   - Accept the fact that you'll make mistakes, *and* you'll learn from them.

   Complete the following exercise.

EXERCISE

Using Cross-Difference Mentoring

Directions: *Make a few notes about how you can make good use of cross-difference mentoring.*

1. What experience have you had with cross-difference mentoring? What did you learn? What, if anything, do you want to do differently next time?

2. If you're currently in a mentoring relationship, how are you and your partner different? How are you similar?

3. What's one goal you have related to cross-difference mentoring?

Glossary of Mentoring Terms

awe factor: exaggerated respect for or admiration of another. We can be in awe of a famous person or someone who seems extraordinary in our eyes. In mentoring, the mentee can be somewhat in awe of a very successful mentor. While respect and a certain amount of deference on the part of the mentee is appropriate, the mentoring pair should take steps to reduce the awe factor. The goal is to create a safe and comfortable relationship in which the mentee feels comfortable reaching out to the mentor and revealing information.

coach: a person who closely observes another's behaviors, breaks down those behaviors into specific discrete steps, and provides suggestions for improving those behaviors. Mentors can be coaches when they have content expertise in a skill.

corrective feedback: reactions aimed at improving an observed behavior. In this **Guide**, giving corrective feedback (as opposed to constructive feedback) is used to differentiate it from the mentoring skill of encouraging (giving positive feedback in the form of praise).

cross-difference mentoring: mentoring that occurs between persons who differ in gender, age, culture, race, background, style (communication, decision making, life), core beliefs, or other significant ways.

development plan: a written outline of development goals, objectives, measures, development activities, resources needed, and a timeline. Often used in a formal mentoring partnership.

enhanced informal mentoring: semi-formal mentoring in the sense that mentors and mentees choose each other and aren't matched or monitored in a program. One or both partners are acquainted with mentoring concepts and strategies and recognize the process as mentoring. Relationship is more focused and guided than completely informal mentoring.

formal mentoring: explicit helping agreements between experienced persons (who may or may not be called mentors) and their mentees. These relationships have goals, formal or informal rules of operating, agreements, and procedures.

inclusion: a safe environment in which people feel valued, respected, and important to each other. They trust one another and can reveal their thoughts and feelings without fear of being rejected, looked down upon, or criticized.

informal mentoring: the unplanned pairings and interactions that occur among experienced and less experienced individuals. Two individuals meet, are drawn to each other, and focus on helping one or both people succeed. The arrangement is informal and may never be recognized as mentoring.

mentee: the person receiving the formal help from a mentor. Synonyms include mentee, mentoree, and protege.

mentor: an experienced person who goes out of his/her way to help another person (the mentee) do two things: (1) set important goals; and (2) build the competencies necessary to achieve them.

mentoree: another word for mentee or protege.

mentoring: the activities and help that mentors give and their mentees receive.

mentorship: a mentoring relationship.

protege: another word for mentee or mentoree. Sometimes the term is written protégé.

reverse mentoring: mentoring in which the roles aren't what they seem at first glance. The person that observers would assume is the mentee is actually the mentor (and vice versa). For example, a young computer wizard acts as a Reverse Mentor to an older, experienced company president (Reverse Mentee).

self-fulfilling prophecy: From R.K. Merton, Columbia University. When one predicts an event or outcome, the expectation changes the behavior of the "prophet" in such a way as to make the event or outcome more likely to happen. Also called the Pygmalion Effect. If a mentor *expects* a mentee to perform well, the mentee will usually do so. The negative effect can also happen. *Application to mentoring*: If the mentor *doesn't* expect much from the mentee or worse, expects failure, the mentor's behavior will reflect this expectation. The mentee can also affect the mentor's performance by expecting good or poor performance.

social efficacy theory: From Albert Bandura, Stanford University. Relates to our belief in our capability to successfully perform in ways that influence events affecting our lives. Our self-efficacy can be increased when we participate in such positive experiences as authentic mastery experiences, observing what models do, and hearing others' positive judgments of us. *Application to mentoring*: mentees should choose to set challenging goals that require them to "master" something. Mentors should allow themselves to be observed and provide genuine and timely positive reinforcement for mentees.

social learning theory: From Albert Bandura, Stanford University. Much of our learning is through observing role models, noting what happens to them, and adjusting our own behavior as a result. In addition, we learn faster and better when we're positively reinforced by persons we respect. *Application to mentoring*: mentees should seek mentors who are respected role models. They should ask for positive reinforcement if their mentors neglect to give it. Mentors should make a point of giving mentees frequent, genuine positive reinforcement.

Resources

1. Barton, K. (2001) *Connecting with Success: How to Build a Mentoring Network to Fast-Forward Your Career*. Palo Alto, CA: Davies-Black Publishing.

2. Bell, C. R. (2002) *Managers as Mentors: Building Partnerships for Learning*. San Francisco: Berrett-Koehler Publishers.

3. Brown, N. S. (1995) *The Role of Mentoring in the Adult Development of Professional Asian-American Women: A Cross-Ethnic Cross-Gender Study*. Dissertation: Pacific Graduate School of Psychology.

4. Collins, E. G. & Scott, P. (1978) Everyone Who Makes It Has a Mentor. *Harvard Business Review,* July-August, 89-101.

5. Covey, S. (1990) *The Seven Habits of Highly Effective People*. New York: Simon & Schuster.

6. Cuomo, M. F. (Ed.) (1999) *The Person Who Changed my Life: Prominent Americans Recall their Mentors*. Secaucus, NJ: Carol Publishing Group.

7. Eagles, Z. E. (1997) *The Nurses' Career Guide: Discovering New Horizons in Health Care*. San Luis Obispo, CA: Sovereignty Press.

8. Fairhurst, G. T. (1996) *The Art of Framing: Managing the Language of Leadership*. San Francisco: Jossey-Bass, Inc. Publishers.

9. Gardner, H. (1996) *Leading Minds: An Anatomy of Leadership*. New York: Basic Books.

10. Goleman, D.; Boyatzis, R.; & McKee, A. (2002) *Primal Leadership: Realizing the Power of Emotional Intelligence*. Boston: Harvard Business School Press.

11. Goleman, D. (1997) *Emotional Intelligence*. New York: Bantam Books.

12. Gray, W. A.; Gray, M. M.; & Anderson, T. D. (1991ff) *Mentoring Style Indicator*. Saanichton, BC: Corporate Mentoring Solutions.

13. Hakim, C. (1994) *We Are All Self-Employed: The New Social Contract for Working in a Changed World*. San Francisco: Berrett-Koehler Publishers.

14. Kouzes, J. M. & Posner, B. Z. (2003) *Encouraging the Heart: A Leader's Guide to Rewarding and Recognizing Others*. San Francisco: Jossey-Bass Inc. Publishers.

15. Kouzes, J. M. & Posner, B. Z. (1990) *The Leadership Challenge: How to Get Extraordinary Things Done in Organizations.* San Francisco: Jossey-Bass Inc. Publishers.

16. Kram, K. E. (1996) Mentoring and Leadership Development, *Journal of Leadership and Organizational Development*, Vol. 17(3), 4-5.

17. Kram, K. E. (1988) *Mentoring at Work: Developmental Relationships in Organizational Life*. Lanham, MD: University Press of America.

18. Kram, K. E. (1983) Phases of the Mentor Relationship. **Academy of Management Journal,** 26 (4), 608-625.

19. McCall, M. W. Jr. (1998) *High Flyers: Developing the Next Generation of Leaders*. Boston: Harvard Business School Press.

20. Moore, A. T. (1995) *Professional African-American Women: Implications for Adult Continuing Education in Career Development*. Dissertation: Northern Illinois University.

21. Murray, M. (2001) *Beyond the Myths and Magic of Mentoring*. San Francisco: Jossey-Bass Inc. Publishers.

22. Murrell, A. J.; Crosby, F. J.; & Ely, R. J. (Eds.) (1999) *Mentoring Dilemmas: Developmental Relationships within Multicultural Organizations.* Mahwah, NJ: Lawrence Erlbaum Associates Inc.

23. Peterson, D. B. & Hicks, M. D. (1996) *Leader as Coach*. Minneapolis: Personnel Decisions International, 800.633.4410.

24. Peterson, D. B. & Hicks, M. D. (1995) *Development FIRST*. Minneapolis: Personnel Decisions International, 800.633.4410.

25. Phillips-Jones, L. (2003) *The Mentee's Guide: How to Have a Successful Relationship with a Mentor*. CCC/The Mentoring Group, 13560 Mesa Drive, Grass Valley, CA 95949, 530.268.1146.

26. Phillips-Jones, L. (2003) *The Mentor's Guide: How to Be the Kind of Mentor You Once Had—Or Wish You'd Had*. CCC/The Mentoring Group, 13560 Mesa Drive, Grass Valley, CA 95949, 530.268.1146.

27. Phillips-Jones, L. (2003) *Planning, Implementing, and Evaluating a Successful Mentoring Initiative: Checklist of Tasks*. CCC/The Mentoring Group, 13560 Mesa Drive, Grass Valley, CA 95949, 530.268.1146.

28. Phillips-Jones, L. (2001 update) *The New Mentors and Proteges: How to Succeed with the New Mentoring Partnerships*. CCC/The Mentoring Group, 13560 Mesa Drive, Grass Valley, CA 95949, 530.268.1146.

29. Phillips-Jones, L. (2003) *Skills for Successful Mentoring: Core Competencies of Outstanding Mentors and Mentees*. CCC/The Mentoring Group, 13560 Mesa Drive, Grass Valley, CA 95949, 530.268.1146.

30. Phillips-Jones, L. (2001) *Strategies for Getting the Mentoring You Need: A Look at Best Practices of Successful Mentees*. CCC/The Mentoring Group, 13560 Mesa Drive, Grass Valley, CA 95949, 530.268.1146.

31. Phillips-Jones, L. (2001) *What Every Manager Should Know about Mentoring: Your Three Mentoring Roles to Help Employees Excel*. CCC/The Mentoring Group, 13560 Mesa Drive, Grass Valley, CA 95949, 530.268.1146.

32. Phillips-Jones, L. (1998) *The Mentoring Skills Assessment (MSA)*. Mind Garden, info@mindgarden.com.

33. Phillips-Jones, L. (1990) Common Problems in Mentoring Relationships, in (Frantzreb, R., Ed.) *Training and Development Yearbook*. Englewood Cliffs, NJ: Prentice Hall.

34. Phillips-Jones, L. (1983) Establishing a Formalized Mentoring Program. *Training and Development Journal*, 37 (2), February, 38, 40-42.

35. Phillips-Jones, L. (1982) *Mentors and Proteges: How to Establish, Strengthen, and Get the Most from a Mentor-Protege Relationship*. New York: Arbor House.

36. Phillips, L. (1977) *Mentors and Proteges*. Unpublished doctoral dissertation. Los Angeles: UCLA.

37. Roberts, A. (1999) Homer's Mentor: Duties Fulfilled or Misconstrued? *History of Education Journal*, Nov.

38. Senge, P. M.; Kleiner, A.; & Roberts, C. (1994) *The Fifth Discipline Fieldbook: Strategies and Tools for Building a Learning Organization*. New York: Currency Doubleday.

39. Senge, P. M. (1994) *The Fifth Discipline: The Art and Practice of the Learning Organization*. New York: Currency Doubleday.

40. Sloman, M. (2002) *The E-Learning Revolution: How Technology is Driving a New Training Paradigm*. New York: American Management Association (AMACOM).

41. Tannen, D. (2001) *Talking From 9 to 5: Women and Men in the Workplace: Language, Sex and Power*. New York: Avon Books.

42. Thomas, D. T. (2001) The Truth about Mentoring Minorities: Race Matters. *Harvard Business Review*, April, 99-107.

43. Tysel, L. C. (1993) *Cross-Gender Mentoring of Successful Women Managers in the United States Government: Toward a Female Model of Mentoring*. Dissertation. Northern Illinois University.

44. Zachary, L. (2000) *The Mentor's Guide: Facilitating Effective Learning Relationships*.

About the Author

Dr. Linda Phillips-Jones is a licensed psychologist, consultant, researcher, and author. She helps organizations design and implement mentoring and other people-development initiatives.

Dr. Phillips-Jones received a Ph.D. in counseling psychology from UCLA, a master's degree from Stanford University, and a bachelor's from the University of Nevada-Reno.

Her 1977 doctoral dissertation was the first on the process and skills of mentoring. Since then, several hundred mentoring dissertations and theses have been written, many referring to this original work. Her first book on mentoring, **MENTORS AND PROTEGES: How to Establish, Strengthen and Get the Most from a Mentor-Protege Relationship** (Arbor House, 1982), has been used worldwide. It was based on her six years of research on more than 500 mentors and proteges and upon her experience as a counseling psychologist and mentoring consultant. **THE NEW MENTORS AND PROTEGES: How to Succeed with the New Mentoring Partnerships** (1992, 1997, 2001 editions) highlights the new twists that mentoring has taken since the eighties and provides new strategies for offering planned mentoring in organizations.

Her mentoring training materials have been used by such organizations as Microsoft Corporation; Hewlett-Packard Company; ITT Industries; Pepperidge Farm; Burlington Northern Santa Fe; Yum Brands; Agilent Technologies; Lucent Technologies; Farmer's Insurance; ConocoPhillips; DuPont; Young Entrepreneurs Organization; Clairol; Varian Techtron (Australia); University of California; Kimberly-Clark; American Family Insurance; Domino's Pizza; Alberta Staff Development (Canada); Canadian Centre for Management Development; the U.S. Departments of Army, Navy, Labor, Justice, Agriculture; California Institute of Technology; and others. She's the author of the *Mentoring Skills Assessment* published by MindGarden.

Dr. Phillips-Jones has been quoted in **The Wall Street Journal, USA Today, Newsday, The Los Angeles Times, The Boston Globe, Success, Psychology Today, New Woman, Glamour, Executive Female, Training and Development Journal, Reader's Digest, Entrepreneur, Black Entrepreneur**, and numerous other print and on-line periodicals.

She's featured as a mentoring expert in the following videos: "Building Bridges: How to Build a Powerful Network," produced by the National Association of Female Executives (NAFE); "Mentoring that Makes a Difference: For Mentors"; "Mentoring that Makes a Difference: For Mentees"; and "Mentoring: The Success Connection." She's presented programs on mentoring at international conferences of the American Society for Training and Development.

Dr. Phillips-Jones was invited to Hungary to teach mentoring as part of an entrepreneurial development program of the U.S. Department of Labor and the Women's Economic Alliance Foundation in Washington. She and her husband, Dr. G. Brian Jones, were invited as foreign experts to teach managerial psychology and organizational behavior in the People's Republic of China and Kenya. She's conducted mentoring training throughout the U.S. and in Canada, England, Scotland, Germany, Australia, Malaysia, Indonesia, Australia, Venezuela, and Hong Kong. During the Vietnam War, she worked five years as a teacher trainer and curriculum designer in South Vietnam.